DWR Java AJAX Applications

A step-by-step example-packed guide to learning professional application development with Direct Web Remoting

Sami Salkosuo

PUBLISHING

BIRMINGHAM - MUMBAI

DWR Java AJAX Applications

First published: October 2008

Production Reference: 1151008

Published by Packt Publishing Ltd.
32 Lincoln Road
Olton
Birmingham, B27 6PA, UK.

ISBN 978-1-847192-93-6

www.packtpub.com

Cover Image by Parag Kadam (Paragvkadam@gmail.com)

Credits

Author

Sami Salkosuo

Reviewers

Jason Crow

Matthew Henry

Sujit Pal

Acquisition Editor

Adil Ahmed

Development Editor

Usha Iyer

Technical Editor

Darshana D. Shinde

Copy Editor

Sumathi Sridhar

Editorial Team Leader

Mithil Kulkarni

Project Manager

Abhijeet Deobhakta

Project Coordinator

Rajashree Hamine

Indexer

Rekha Nair

Proofreader

Chris Smith

Production Coordinator

Rajni R. Thorat

Cover Work

Rajni R. Thorat

About the Author

Sami Salkosuo is a Software IT Architect at IBM Software Group, Finland. He has over ten years of experience in Java, Web, and integration technologies.

Sami has written several articles for IBM developerWorks, and is also the co-author of an IBM Redbook: *Portalizing Domino Applications*.

I am thankful to the reviewers Sujit Pal, Matthew Henry, and Jason Crow for their comments that helped me improve my writing. My thanks to Rajashree Hamine, Usha Iyer, Darshana Shinde, and others at Packt Publishing for making this book come true.

My sincere thanks also for my family for their patience and support.

About the Reviewers

Jason Crow is the lead Java Developer for Office Depot, Inc. in Delray Beach, Florida. He specializes in blending his expertise in Java, DWR, HTML, CSS, and jQuery to enhance usability and to bring dynamic features to officedepot.com. He actively contributes back to the community through his blog `http://greatwebguy.com`.

Matthew Henry is the Programming Services Manager at LeTourneau University. Matthew has worked in IT and computer related fields as a programmer for 30 years. Matthew co-authored *Upgrading to Lotus Notes 7* and has written various articles for specific computer industry magazines.

Sujit Pal started programming some 20 years ago, and has never looked back since. He currently works at Healthline Networks, Inc., a search vertical focused on health, as part of its Research and Development team. Apart from his work, his favorite pastime is to explore new software technologies, techniques, and languages, and he writes about his experiments at `sujitpal.blogspot.com`.

Table of Content

Preface

AJAX enables a rich desktop-like user interface in the browser and enables interactive interfaces that can even replace traditional user interfaces. Communication between browser and server is done in the background and because only the data is transferred between the browser and the server, AJAX applications seem to be, and are actually, fast and responsive to the users.

DWR, Direct Web Remoting, is an Open Source Java framework, licensed under the commercial-friendly Apache Software License v2 for building AJAX applications. DWR's main idea is to hide AJAX implementation details, like XMLHttpRequest and such, from developers. Developers can concentrate on developing the application and business objects and leave the AJAX details behind the scenes where they belong.

DWR allows server-side Java classes to be used in the browser (it's like an RPC between JavaScript functions and the server-side Java) and also allows JavaScript functions to be used in the server (Reverse AJAX). DWR dynamically generates JavaScript functions from Java classes via XML-based configuration, which can be called from browser via the DWR JavaScript library. A DWR servlet on the server side receives requests and calls the actual Java implementation. DWR includes a couple of JavaScript libraries that are required for DWR to work, and are also helpful for developers.

The term Reverse AJAX is used when a server is used to query and/or control the client browser behavior. DWR supports three different methods to do reverse AJAX in applications: Piggyback, Polling (by the client), and Comet (server push).

You may have an on-going project where you may want to use a framework such as JSF or Spring for building the whole solution. In these cases, AJAX and DWR are just a part of the overall picture, and so DWR needs to integrate with other frameworks nicely, and does that successfully!

The DWR project has thought about security very thoroughly. The DWR framework has taken into account many security issues and there is a lot of discussion about security at the DWR website.

This book is written for professional Java developers who are interested in learning DWR and AJAX framework. It starts with a tutorial on DWR's main features and functions. Then it covers setting up the development environment. It concludes with some sample applications.

The later chapters are full of example code for sample applications, to aid comprehension.

What This Book Covers

Chapter 1 is a brief introduction to AJAX technology and DWR. It also discusses the DWR community and describes briefly what information can be found about DWR on the Internet.

Chapter 2 describes DWR features that we use in the samples of this book — a high-level view of how DWR makes a developer's life easier. It discusses reverse AJAX, DWR JavaScript libraries, converters, creators, filters, and signatures. It also contains a section on integrating DWR with other projects and another on security.

Chapter 3 sets the stage for development by describing how to set up the development environment and how to test and debug our sample applications. It covers DWR-supported browsers and environments, configuration, error handling, packaging, and deployment.

Chapter 4 is the first chapter dedicated to sample code. The examples in this chapter include typical user interface elements such as tables and lists, and how they can be implemented using DWR. It also has an example for field completion.

Chapter 5 discusses how to use DWR in more advanced user interface elements such as forms, navigation tree, and scrolling a map.

Chapter 6 shows how DWR applications are integrated to a database, a web service, or a messaging system.

Chapter 7 includes two sample applications: Collaborative Book Authoring, which shows how DWR is used to create a web based multi-user authoring environment, and Chatroom — a typical multi-user chat room application using DWR.

What You Need for This Book

This book is for professional Java developers and architects who want to learn about DWR by examples. Several skills are needed or are beneficial to get the most out of this book.

First of all, Java development skills are needed. Especially web development using Java technologies like Java Enterprise Edition (JEE), Servlets, and JSPs. Experience about other web technologies like JavaScript, HTML, and CSS is also useful.

Eclipse tooling should be familiar and other useful skills are knowledge about JEE application servers and experience about common technologies like XML.

Knowledge about the basics of AJAX technology is helpful. However, the basics of AJAX are introduced in this book.

Who is This Book For

This book is written for competent Java developers and assumes that you are a professional rather than a hobbyist. You should be familiar with the concepts of programming, Web 2.0, and AJAX.

Conventions

In this book, you will find a number of styles of text that distinguish between different kinds of information. Here are some examples of these styles, and an explanation of their meaning.

Code words in text are shown as follows: "We can include other contexts through the use of the `include` directive."

A block of code will be set as follows:

```
<?xml version="1.0" encoding="UTF-8"?>
<!DOCTYPE dwr PUBLIC
    "-//GetAhead Limited//DTD Direct Web Remoting 2.0//EN"
    "http://getahead.org/dwr/dwr20.dtd">
<dwr>
  <allow>
    <create creator="new" javascript="HorizontalMenu">
      <param name="class" value="samples.HorizontalMenu" />
    </create>
  </allow>
</dwr>
```

When we wish to draw your attention to a particular part of a code block, the relevant lines or items will be made bold:

```java
public boolean submitOrder(String name, String address,
                        String creditCardNumber, String expiryDate)
{
    CreditCardValidatorSoapProxy ccValidatorProxy =
                        new CreditCardValidatorSoapProxy();
    int rv = -1;
    try {
        rv = ccValidatorProxy.validCard(creditCardNumber,
                                expiryDate.replace("/", ""));
        if (rv != 0) {
            System.out.println("Credit card check failed: " + rv);
        }
    } catch (RemoteException e) {
        e.printStackTrace();
    }
    if(rv==0)
    {
        //credit card valid, submit to order system
        new OrderSystem(name,address,creditCardNumber,expiryDate);
    }
    return rv == 0;
}
```

Any command-line input and output is written as follows:

```
deploy -user system -password manager deploy d:\temp\HelloWorldServlet.war
```

New terms and **important words** are introduced in a bold-type font. Words that you see on the screen, in menus or dialog boxes for example, appear in our text like this: "clicking the **Next** button moves you to the next screen".

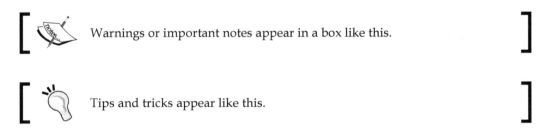

Warnings or important notes appear in a box like this.

Tips and tricks appear like this.

Reader Feedback

Feedback from our readers is always welcome. Let us know what you think about this book, what you liked or may have disliked. Reader feedback is important for us to develop titles that you really get the most out of.

To send us general feedback, simply drop an email to feedback@packtpub.com, making sure to mention the book title in the subject of your message.

If there is a book that you need and would like to see us publish, please send us a note in the **SUGGEST A TITLE** form on www.packtpub.com or email suggest@packtpub.com.

If there is a topic that you have expertise in and you are interested in either writing or contributing to a book, see our author guide on www.packtpub.com/authors.

Customer Support

Now that you are the proud owner of a Packt book, we have a number of things to help you to get the most from your purchase.

Downloading the Example Code for the Book

Visit http://www.packtpub.com/files/code/2936_Code.zip to directly download the example code.

 The downloadable files contain instructions on how to use them.

Errata

Although we have taken every care to ensure the accuracy of our contents, mistakes do happen. If you find a mistake in one of our books—maybe a mistake in text or code—we would be grateful if you would report this to us. By doing this you can save other readers from frustration, and help to improve subsequent versions of this book. If you find any errata, report them by visiting http://www.packtpub.com/support, selecting your book, clicking on the **let us know** link, and entering the details of your errata. Once your errata are verified, your submission will be accepted and the errata added to the list of existing errata. The existing errata can be viewed by selecting your title from http://www.packtpub.com/support.

Piracy

Piracy of copyright material on the Internet is an ongoing problem across all media. At Packt, we take the protection of our copyright and licenses very seriously. If you come across any illegal copies of our works in any form on the Internet, please provide the location address or website name immediately so we can pursue a remedy.

Please contact us at copyright@packtpub.com with a link to the suspected pirated material.

We appreciate your help in protecting our authors, and our ability to bring you valuable content.

Questions

You can contact us at questions@packtpub.com if you are having a problem with some aspect of the book, and we will do our best to address it.

1
Introduction

Learning by doing is a key if you want to benefit from this book. Since the target audience is the developer community, much of this book consists of examples using DWR in action. Chapters 1 to 3 introduce the main features of DWR, and discuss how to get the development work started. Chapters 4 to 7 are full of sample code, and focus on the source code samples and applications.

This chapter introduces AJAX technology and a widely used Java framework for building AJAX applications: **Direct Web Remoting**, commonly known as **DWR**. The introductory sections on both AJAX and DWR are brief since AJAX is already a well-known technology and most of us have at least heard about it and know what it stands for. The introduction to DWR is presented in a short "executive summary" before we dive into more details and examples on DWR in the later chapters.

The following sections are discussed in this chapter:

- What is AJAX?
- DWR: AJAX for Java Developers
- The DWR Community

What is AJAX?

AJAX is the abbreviation for **Asynchronous JavaScript and XML**. This gives an almost comprehensive explanation of the technology, except that XML is not required. The term AJAX surfaced around February 2005 and was first used by Jesse James Garrett (http://www.adaptivepath.com/ideas/essays/archives/000385.php), long after the building blocks of AJAX, JavaScript and XML, were available and in wide use.

The principle idea of AJAX is in the word "Asynchronous". This feature enables rich a desktop-like user interface in the browser and enables interactive interfaces that can even replace traditional user interfaces. Communication between browser and server is done in the background. Moreover, as only the data is transferred between the browser and the server, AJAX applications are actually fast and responsive to users. The following figures display how a typical request-response application works (upper diagram), and how AJAX applications work compared to the request-response application (lower diagram).

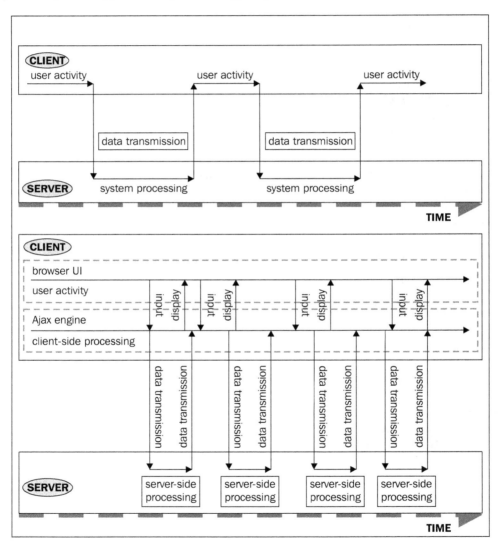

The main component of AJAX technology is XmlHttpRequest, which is a JavaScript object, first supported by Mozilla in 2002. The concept was originally developed by Microsoft in 1999 for Internet Explorer 5.0 and it was then called XMLHTTP. The following link provides the details and history of XmlHttpRequest: http://en.wikipedia.org/wiki/XMLHttpRequest.

XmlHttpRequest is used to transfer data between client and server asynchronously. The following figure shows the AJAX sequence diagram and how XmlHttpRequest is used:

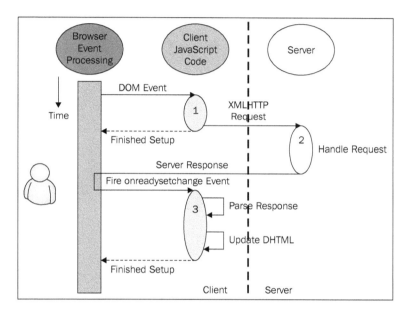

AJAX is dealt with in detail in many books such as *Head Rush Ajax*, a "brain friendly guide" to AJAX and also on Internet sites. Further, the assumption is that most of you already know AJAX and you are reading this book for reasons other than just learning AJAX basics.

DWR: AJAX for Java Developers

Direct Web Remoting (http://www.directwebremoting.org), is an Open Source Java framework, licensed under commercial-friendly Apache Software License v2 (http://www.apache.org/licenses/LICENSE-2.0.html) for building AJAX applications. DWR's main idea is to hide AJAX implementation details such as XMLHttpRequest from developers. Developers can concentrate on developing the application and business objects and leave AJAX details behind the scenes where they belong.

DWR allows server-side Java classes to be used in a browser (it's like RPC between JavaScript functions and server-side Java) and also allows JavaScript functions to be used in a server (Reverse AJAX). Through an XML-based configuration, DWR dynamically generates JavaScript functions of Java classes, which can be called from the browser via a DWR JavaScript library. A DWR servlet on the server side receives requests and calls the actual Java implementation.

The following figure displays the positioning of DWR in user applications and is taken from the DWR website (http://directwebremoting.org/dwr/overview/dwr).

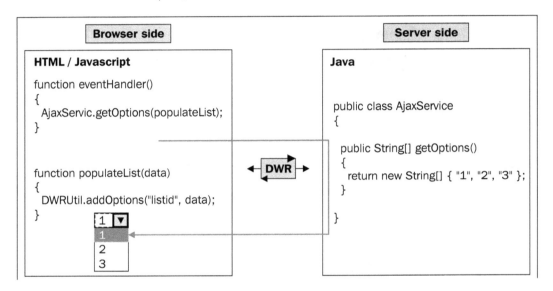

In the previous figure, the JavaScript **function eventHandler()** responds to some browser event like clicking a button. Event handlers use the **AjaxService** object and call the **getOptions()** method just as if **AjaxService** were a normal JavaScript object. A developer can implement client-side and server-side code and leave the communication between the client and the server to DWR.

Calling server-side Java from JavaScript causes a lot of things to happen and also requires a lot to happen behind the scenes:

- When a DWR-enabled web page is requested, DWR dynamically generates JavaScript functions from Java classes based on configuration.

  When the **function eventHandler()** gets called, say when clicking a button, the developer calls a dynamically generated function (**AjaxService. getOptions(populateList)** as shown in the previous figure) and the DWR JavaScript library takes the parameters, serializes them, and calls the DWR servlet on the server.

- The DWR servlet receives a request and, based on configuration, the servlet instantiates a Java object such as **AjaxService**, and calls the required method, for example, **AjaxService.getOptions(populateList)**.

- When the Java method is finished, the return value (a String array) is returned to the DWR servlet, and servlet serializes the return value and sends the response to the DWR JavaScript function on the browser.

- The DWR JavaScript function receives the response on the browser and based on the parameter, **populateList** (this is the name of the callback function in the **AjaxService.getOptions()** function), DWR calls the **populateList** function with the return value from the Java method as the parameter. The **AjaxService.getOptions()** JavaScript function is generated dynamically by DWR, and it communicates with the DWR servlet behind the scenes.

- The callback function (written by the developer) does the desired thing with the return value such as updating the browser page and adding new options to the drop-down field.

DWR is well-suited for Java developers, because this kind of approach is very easy to get into.

The DWR Community

DWR has very active mailing lists available for DWR users:

- Java.net (`https://dwr.dev.java.net/servlets/SummarizeList?listName=users`)

- Nabble (`http://www.nabble.com/DWR---Users-f13934.html`)

- Gmane (`http://dir.gmane.org/gmane.comp.java.dwr.user`)

These mailing lists have lots of information, which would be helpful to any DWR user, and any one can participate in them.

There is a mailing list available for DWR security, where DWR security issues are discussed. In order to participate, application to list must be made separately and it must include corporate email addresses and titles or other means of identification. Separate applications are made so that DWR security issues can be discussed without public dessemination (it is not intended to keep security issues a secret). Application to join security mailing list can be done from `http://groups.google.com/group/dwr-security`

DWR development mailing list are as follows:

- Java.net (`https://dwr.dev.java.net/servlets/SummarizeList?listName=dev`)
- Nabble (`http://www.nabble.com/DWR---Dev-f13937.html`)

he blog of DWR creator Joe Walker (`http://directwebremoting.org/blog/joe`) includes news about DWR and thoughts about web development.

Commercial support is also available from SitePen (`http://sitepen.com/services/support.php`). There are several support packages available, and there are also possibilities to customize support packages to specific needs.

DWR is used by thousands of developers, and it has been used by companies such as American Airlines, Walmart, Citigroup, Mastercard, and many others. DWR is used both in public sites and Intranet sites.

DWR is also part of the Dojo Foundation, which is an independent legal entity that provides infrastructure for development. The members include IBM and SitePen. In addition to DWR, Dojo Foundation also sponsors Dojo Toolkit, OpenRecord, and Cometd projects. The following website has more information about the Dojo Foundation:

`http://dojotoolkit.org/foundation`

Summary

This chapter briefly introduced AJAX and DWR. AJAX is a fundamental technology that uses browser-based JavaScript to build Internet applications with better user experience than typical request-response web applications.

DWR is a Java framework for building AJAX applications, and it is targeted mainly at Java developers who don't want to implement the low-level "stuff" that makes AJAX work.

The rest of the book is about DWR features and sample code that can be used in your own projects. The examples provided in the later chapters show some of the common situations in which to use DWR and how to use it.

2
DWR Features

This chapter describes some main features of DWR: Reverse AJAX, security, DWR JavaScript libraries, and DWR's integration with other projects.

Reverse AJAX is basically a method to call client-side JavaScript from server-side Java classes. The security section discusses what has been done in DWR in order to prevent unwanted access to the server by exploiting DWR features.

DWR includes a couple of useful JavaScript libraries that are explained here together with how to use DWR with other projects, such as Struts or JSF.

This chapter covers the following sections:

- Ease of Use — A high-level view of how DWR makes a developer's life easier
- Reverse AJAX — Describes what Reverse AJAX means
- DWR JavaScript Libraries — Describes the JavaScript libraries that come with DWR: `engine.js`, `util.js`, and `gi.js`
- Converters — Presents how DWR marshals/unmarshals objects
- Creators, Filters, and Signatures — Introduces important DWR configuration elements
- Integration with Other Projects — Briefly describes how DWR integrates with other projects
- Security — Gives an overview of DWR security

In addition to the features described in this chapter, DWR features such as error handling and configuration are presented in Chapter 3, *Getting Started*.

Ease of Use

The main feature of DWR is its ease of use. DWR hides a lot of details from developers. This means that we can use AJAX functionality and we don't need to know about XmlHttpRequest for example, or how to send a Java object to a browser and so on. DWR has its own framework for performing the required marshaling/unmarshaling of Java objects to JavaScript and vice versa.

The setup for DWR consists of copying the dwr.jar file to the **WEB-INF | lib** directory in the application WAR file, and installing the application in the server before starting to use it. There are no special interfaces to implement in our own Java classes and it is even possible to develop a Java object completely transparently, so that the object doesn't know any DWR-specific classes. DWR provides well-documented APIs for us to use, and we can take advantage of it when developing, for example, Reverse AJAX applications.

And finally we can leverage the existing Java skills because DWR does not force us to replace the existing code, but instead lives side by side with non-AJAX applications and allows us to gradually change the required parts of an application to AJAX functionality.

Reverse AJAX

The term Reverse AJAX is used when a server is used to query and/or control a client-browser behavior. This may cause some questions because it sounds like our browsers are now vulnerable to attack while we visit the web pages of the world.

Luckily that is not the case, because it is not possible for a server to open a connection to a browser. A browser must always be the initiator of the connection. So, the question about security is actually valid, but a problem would mean that the website in question is designed and implemented for causing harm.

DWR supports three different methods to do Reverse AJAX in applications: Piggyback, Polling (by the client), and Comet (server push).

Piggyback

The piggyback method works so that whenever a server has an update to be sent to the client, it waits until the client opens a connection and requests some content from the server. When that happens, the server includes a new update with the response, and it is delivered to the client where DWR recognizes the update and acts accordingly and makes the update on the user's web page.

The Piggyback method is the default method for Reverse AJAX in DWR and it is called Passive Reverse AJAX (the other methods are called Active Reverse AJAX) and requires no configuration. For busy developers like us it is often a good enough solution (by the way, learning when to stop and when to develop "good-enough software" is one step from journeyman to master; see *The Pragmatic Programmer: From Journeyman to Master*, by Andrew Hunt and David Thomas)

A downside to Piggyback is that any update that happens on the server side may take a long time before it is visible to users. Depending on the application, this may not be a problem, but if it is, then the other two methods may be used, Polling and Comet, which are Active Reverse AJAX methods.

Using Reverse AJAX requires the use of DWR classes in the application code on the server side. DWR has a class called `ScriptProxy` that is used to execute JavaScript functions on the client. As an example, the following code snippet, which could be in a remote Java method, gets all the script sessions (in essence, HTTP sessions but for scripts) for a given page, `mainpage.jsp`, and then adds a function call that gets called in all the clients that are known to the server and have the `mainpage.jsp` open.

```
Collection<ScriptSession> sessions = serverContext.getScriptSessionsBy
Page(contextPath + "/mainpage.jsp");
ScriptProxy proxy = new ScriptProxy(sessions);
proxy.addFunctionCall("newMessage",newMessage);
```

On the `mainpage.jsp`, we would have the following function, `newMessage`, that updates some field in the web page.

```
function newMessage(newMessageParam)
{
    elementToBeUpdated=document.getElementById("messageArea");
    elementToBeUpdated.innerHTML=newMessageParam;
}
```

No configuration is needed when using Reverse AJAX using the Piggyback method. It is enabled by default in DWR. When using Piggyback, clients receive updates after they make an AJAX (DWR) request to the server application. DWR then sends all updates (from Reverse AJAX methods) together with the actual response to the client where DWR updates the web page (as in the previous example).

Polling

Polling is a "no-brainer" way to do Reverse AJAX, although it really isn't reverse since DWR periodically polls the server if there are any events on the server side of the application that require updates to the web page.

This method may be good in some cases, especially when there is no issue about extra load on the network and the server that polling causes or when updates to a client do not need to be (near) real-time as in Comet.

When we use the Polling method for Reverse AJAX the code is the same as in the sample code in the Piggyback section. Only the configuration needs to be changed. In order to use Polling we need to configure DWR to Active Reverse AJAX. This is done by adding the following init parameter to the DWR servlet in the web.xml file.

```
<init-param>
  <param-name>activeReverseAjaxEnabled</param-name>
  <param-value>true</param-value>
</init-param>
```

We also need to enable web pages for Reverse AJAX. This is done by adding the following line to a web page that we are using to receive Reverse AJAX requests from the server.

```
dwr.engine.setActiveReverseAjax(true);
```

The above configuration is actually all that we need for using the Comet method, which can be seen in the following section. For the Polling method, we need an additional init parameter in the web.xml file:

```
<init-param>
  <param-name>org.directwebremoting.extend.ServerLoadMonitor
                                       </param- name>
  <param-value>org.directwebremoting.impl.PollingServerLoadMonitor
                                       </param-value>
</init-param>
```

There is also the optional init parameter for specifying the poll interval. The default interval is 5 seconds, and it can be changed with the following init parameter.

```
<init-param>
  <param-name>disconnectedTime</param-name>
  <param-value>60000</param-value>
</init-param>
```

Comet

Comet, known to some as long-lived HTTP, is a very recent term (used first by Alex Russell in March 2006 http://alex.dojotoolkit.org/?p=545) for a server push method, where the browser opens the connection and it is kept open so that the server can push updates to the browser when needed, and the latency for updates is very low. The following figure shows how Comet compares to the normal AJAX model:

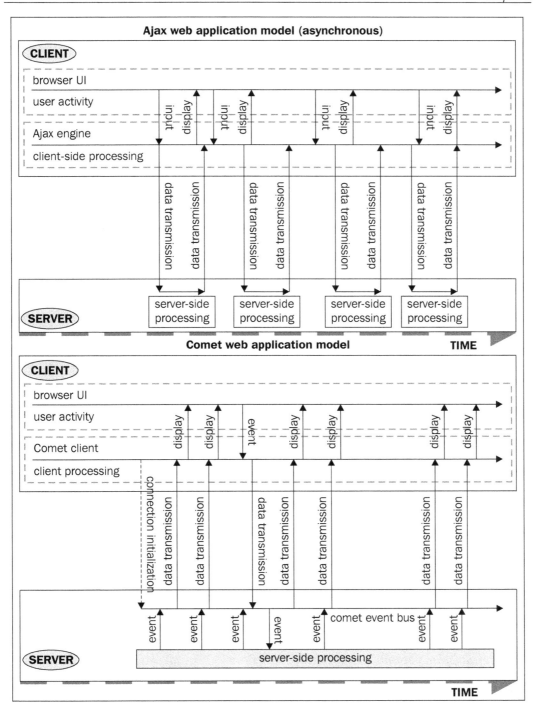

As we can see from the figure, Comet enables the server to send updates in response to the events, almost in real–time, and there is no need to wait for the user to open a connection or to use Polling.

As mentioned in the previous section, Comet requires only the enabling of Active Reverse AJAX in the `init` parameter and the enabling of Reverse AJAX in the web page. Active Reverse AJAX using Comet has two modes: Full Streaming Mode (default in DWR 2.0.3 and earlier versions) and Early Closing Mode (default in DWR 2.0.4 and later versions).

The Full Streaming Mode has the fastest response time and it enables near real-time responses to the client when an event occurs on the server. In this mode, every 60 seconds, DWR checks whether the browser is active or not by closing the connection and reopening it. Early Closing Mode on the other hand causes DWR to close the connection when browser receives the output and then to reopen it. For Early Closing Mode, there is the `init` parameter called `maxWaitAfterWrite` and its value is the time in milliseconds to wait before closing the connection (and reopening it) after receiving input from the server.

There are a couple of issues that should be remembered while using Comet in DWR applications, especially for applications that have a large number of users. As clients keep the connections open to the server, it is possible that the server resources are consumed for connections and their threads. This increases the infrastructure requirements for the DWR application unnecessarily. The solution is to use the `maxWaitAfterWrite` `init` parameter and tweak it to an appropriate value. Other solutions are to use Polling or Passive Reverse AJAX.

In all the three methods, Piggyback, Polling, and Comet, DWR shows its strengths because we don't really have to know the implementation details of Reverse AJAX. DWR handles them behind the scenes and hides the details of Comet and the Polling methods, and we can use any of the three methods by just configuring DWR in the correct manner.

DWR JavaScript Libraries

DWR includes a few JavaScript libraries that are required for DWR to work and that are also helpful for developers: `engine.js`, `util.js`, and `gi.js`.

The first JavaScript library, `engine.js`, is the core of DWR's browser-side functionality, and is required for all the pages that use AJAX and DWR. The second library, `util.js`, contains useful utility functions but is not required for DWR. And the third library, `gi.js`, is used to integrate DWR with TIBCO **General Interface** (**GI**) for AJAX Applications.

engine.js

The `engine.js` library is mandatory for DWR applications since it has functions to marshal calls from the dynamically generated JavaScript functions to remote Java classes in the server. The following fragment must be present in all HTML pages that need DWR functionality:

```
<script type='text/javascript' src='/<web app name>/dwr/engine.js'>
</script>
```

There are a number of options and methods in the `engine.js` library. The functions in the library are prefixed by `dwr.engine`, and the library also has methods to set handler functions for errors and warnings.

DWR is designed to use the correct options (and methods) automatically, so in many cases, we don't need to set any options. However, setting options may sometimes be necessary. Especially when browsers do not behave as expected and we have to work around browser quirks, we may need to set some options.

Some of the options are related to how DWR handles the actual call from the browser to the server. One option is `"async"` and its value is either true or false. If we set `async` to false, then DWR will contact the server synchronously as shown in the following example.

```
NavigationTree.getChildren(value,{
  async:false,
  callback:function(childElements)
  {
    for (index in childElements)
    {
      ....
    }
  }
});
```

The above example generates a navigation tree (see the sample in Chapter 5) when a page is loaded. If loading is asynchronous, functionality would be affected because an asynchronous operation would make the results unpredictable and the user experience would deteriorate considerably. The `engine.js` library is also used to set the pre-and post-hook functions that are executed before the remote call and after the remote call is finished. This feature is useful for debugging and also if we need to do modifications to the user interface, such as disabling components. Post hooks are used for enabling components disabled in the pre-hook function. The following code sets the `PreHook` and `PostHook` functions that alert the user whenever DWR makes a request.

```
dwr.engine.setPreHook(requestStart);
dwr.engine.setPostHook(requestEnd);

function requestStart()
{
  alert('Request start');
}

function requestEnd()
{
  alert('Request end');
}
```

Other features of `engine.js` include the possibility to call the server in a batch with one or more remote functions that are called together. The following code calls three remoted methods in a batch with a timeout of 5 seconds.

```
dwr.engine.beginBatch();
WorldMap.getEvents(callback:function(results){…});
WorldMap.getArea(coordinates, showPreview);
WorldMap.sendEvents(events, result);
dwr.engine.endBatch({
  timeout:5000
});
```

DWR also has a feature called 'call ordering'. When it is enabled, responses to remote calls are received in the order they were sent. By default, call ordering is not enabled and if it is enabled, it may slow down the application. If call ordering is needed, it is enabled by adding `dwr.engine.setOrdered(true)` to the web page and it affects to all DWR calls within that web page.

util.js

The `util.js` library contains many useful JavaScript functions that can be used in our applications. This library is designed to be used even without the rest of DWR since it does not need full DWR functionality (with one exception: the `useLoadingMessage()` function).

The library has functions to manipulate HTML elements including tables, lists, and images. The following is a table of functions found in `util.js` with short descriptions of each.

Function	Syntax	Description
`addOptions`	`dwr.util.addOptions(id, [ "one", "two", "three" ])`	Allows addition of elements without page refresh to lists and select elements (ol, ul, and select) specified by ID.
`addRows`	`dwr.util.addRows (id, array, cellfuncs, [options])`	Adds rows to a specified table element. array parameter is used to populate data so that there is one row per array element. Pseudo-code for creating a table looks like this: `for each member in array` `for each function in cellfuncs` `create cell from cellfunc(array[i])`
`byId`	`dwr.util.byId()`	This function finds the element in the current HTML document with the given ID. This may be used instead of the `document.getElementById` JavaScript function.
`getValue()`	`dwr.util.getValue(id)`	Gets value from HTML elements such as div and input elements.
`getText()`	`dwr.util.getText(id)`	Designed for select lists and returns the displayed text instead of the value of the current option.
`getValues()`	`dwr.util.getValues ({ div:null, textarea: null})`	This function gets the values of specified elements. The function parameter is a map where the key is an HTML element ID and the value holds the element value after this function is executed.

Function	Syntax	Description

onReturn()	dwr.util.onReturn(event, submitFunction)	Useful function to catch an event when return is pressed on a text element. This works on text elements where the onkeypress or onkeydown event is tied to the onReturn function:
		
		`<input type="text"`
		`    onkeypress="dwr.`
		`util.onReturn(event,`
		`submitFunction)"/>`
		
		`<input type="button"`
		`onclick="submitFunct`
		`ion()"/>`

removeAllOptions()	dwr.util.removeAllOptions(id);	Removes all options from ul, ol, or select elements specified by an ID.
removeAllRows()	dwr.util.removeAllRows(id)	Removes all rows from a table specified by an ID.
selectRange()	dwr.util.selectRange(id,start,end)	Selects a range of text in an input box between the start and end positions.
setValue()	dwr.util.setValue(id,value)	Sets the value of specified HTML element. Works with most of the HTML elements, most importantly input elements and divs.
setValues()	dwr.util.setValues({name:value})	Is similar to setValue(), but the function parameter is an object with name/value pairs. The name is the ID of the HTML element and the value is the new value of the element.

Function	Syntax	Description

toDescriptiveString()	`dwr.util.`
	`toDescriptiveString`
	`(id,detailLevel,options)`
		A useful pretty-print function that prints a JavaScript object in human-readable form, with the possibility to choose the level detail.

useLoadingMessage()	`dwr.util.` `useLoadingMessage()`	DWR-specific loading message that shows "loading" on the top right corner of the web page.

The descriptions in the table are just for reference. The DWR samples in the following chapters show how to use these utility functions and the DWR homepage explains these functions in more detail. And, of course, JavaScript source code is available for those who are interested in looking into details.

One parameter option that is worth mentioning for functions is `escapeHTML:false`. By default, `escapeHTML` is true and means that all HTML elements are escaped (especially `<`, `>`, `&`, double quote, and single quote; this is to prevent cross-site scripting attacks).

gi.js

The `gi.js` library helps to integrate DWR with TIBCO General Interface (GI) for AJAX Applications, an Open Source library that includes dozens of ready-made AJAX components as well as tools to help the development of AJAX applications using TIBCO General Interface.

DWR's `gi.js` provides useful functions to integrate with TIBCO GI such as `dwr.gi.toCdfDocument()`, which generates **CDF** (**Common Data Format**) documents from JavaScript objects. CDF is TIBCO GI's common format that allows sharing data among TIBCO GI components, performing data mapping and transfering data between client controls.

More information about TIBCO GI is found on the TIBCO Developer Network, `http://www.tibco.com/devnet/gi/default.jsp`.

Converters

Converters are DWR's means of marshaling data back and forth from the client to the server. There are many basic converters that are enabled by default, and it is also possible to create new converters.

Basic converters include converters for all primitive types, strings, and the following objects:

- From `java.lang` package: `Boolean`, `Byte`, `Short`, `Integer`, `Long`, `Float`, `Double`, `Character`
- From `java.math` package: `BigInteger` and `BigDecimal`
- DateConverter for `java.util.Date`, and classes from `java.sql` package: `Date`, `Times`, and `Timestamp`

DWR also has converters for arrays (of all aforementioned objects), Java Beans and Objects, collections (`Map` and `Collection`), DOM objects, Enums, and others such as the Servlet objects and Hibernate beans.

The DWR API has a `Converter` interface that can be implemented for custom converters. This is not used very often because `BeanConverter` works for many custom objects if they are coded according to the `JavaBean` specification.

Creators, Filters, and Signatures

Creators are used by DWR to instantiate our remote objects on the server side. Chapter 3 has a section about Creators, and how to use them.

Filters are used to intercept calls to remote objects. Interception can occur before or after the call, and filters can be used for various purposes such as logging, security, parameter checking, or even adding extra latency to the DWR calls. The following samples shows simple filter code, and how it is configured in `dwr.xml` for a single class:

```
public class NotifyRestrictedAccessFilter {
public Object doFilter(Object obj, Method method, Object[] params,
AjaxFilterChain chain) throws Exception {
    //if params include monitored sentence
    //then send mail to security officials
    … code here …
    return chain.doFilter(obj, method, params);
  }
}

<allow>
<create creator="new"javascript="GetAreaDetails">
    <param name="class" value="org.area.NumberedArea"/>
    <filter class="org.filters.NotifyRestrictedAccessFilter"/>
</create>
  ...
</allow>
```

Signatures are specified in `dwr.xml`, and they are used to instruct DWR to correctly operate on types that are included in collections such as `java.util.List`. For example, if we have a remote method with the signature `void setAdressses(List addresses)`, DWR has no way of finding out that the type contained in a list is `String`. That is why we need the following signature in `dwr.xml` to instruct DWR to behave correctly.

```
<signatures>
  <![CDATA[
  import java.util.List;
  import myclasses.AllAddresses;
  AllAddresses.setAddresses(List<String> allAddresses);
  ]]>
</signatures>
```

Integration with Other Projects

Often, DWR is not used just by itself. Perhaps, you have an on-going project where decision has been made to use a framework such as JSF or Spring for building the whole solution. In these cases, AJAX and DWR are just a part of the overall picture, and so DWR needs to integrate with other projects nicely. And that it does.

DWR integrates with the following:

- JSF (`http://java.sun.com/javaee/javaserverfaces/`), Java Server Faces for building user interfaces
- Spring (`http://www.springframework.org/`), a complete Java/JEE application framework
- WebWork (`http://www.opensymphony.com/webwork/`), a web application development framework
- Hibernate (`http://www.hibernate.org/`), an object/relational persistence and query service
- Integration to a portal such as Apache Jetspeed using JSR 168 portlets is also doable; for example, see the article on IBM developerWorks (`http://www.ibm.com/developerworks/java/library/j-ajaxportlet/`)
- And many others, whose integrations are provided by DWR or the other projects itself

Explaining all the integrations here is out of scope but, as an example, JSF integration is pretty straightforward.

DWR includes two extension points for JSF integration; one is `JsfCreator`, which is used to access `ManagedBeans` of the JSF from the DWR application and the other is DWR/Faces servlet filter, which allows us to access Java beans from `FacesContext`.

The filter needs to be configured in the web.xml file in order to use JsfCreator:

```
<filter>
  <filter-name>DwrFacesFilter</filter-name>
  <filter-class>uk.ltd.getahead.dwr.servlet.FacesExtensionFilter
  </filter-class>
</filter>

<filter-mapping>
  <filter-name>DwrFacesFilter</filter-name>
  <url-pattern>/dwr/*</url-pattern>
</filter-mapping>
```

In the dwr.xml, file we insert the JSF ManagedBeans configuration:

```
<allow>
  . . .
  <create creator="jsf" javascript="ScriptName">
    <param name="managedBeanName" value="beanName"/>
    <param name="class" value="your.class"/>
  </create>
  . . .
</allow>
```

After the configuration, we are able to use JSF ManagedBeans from the DWR application.

Security

Security is always important, and the DWR project has thought about security very thoroughly. The DWR framework has taken into account many security issues, and there is lots of discussion about security on the DWR website, enough to fill several books about the subject.

Among the people for whom security is important are developers like you and me. Software does only what we instruct it to do, so we must be conscious about security during development and do our best to limit the possibilities to exploit our work.

While using DWR, we manually specify in the dwr.xml configuration (unless we have created some automatic code-generation software that does it for us) which Java classes and methods we want to remote to JavaScript. This way we can be sure that no attacker can exploit any other objects than our explicitly remoted Java objects (and we can concentrate to make those objects as secure as possible).

The configuration in `dwr.xml` also includes a `create` entry for each remoted Java class. We can use singleton, or new, or some other mechanism. We can also limit which methods are allowed using the include and exclude elements in `dwr.xml`. There are also security parameters in the `web.xml` configuration file such as `allowScriptTagRemoting` and `crossDomainSessionSecurity`, which when enabled, may be a huge security risk. So make sure you understand what you are doing if you are enabling the parameters.

There is one configuration parameter that is very useful while developing a DWR application, but that is a security risk in the production (especially public) site. The following `init-param`, `debug`, and `test mode` can be added in the `web.xml`.

```
<init-param>
  <param-name>debug</param-name>
  <param-value>true</param-value>
</init-param>
```

When `debug`/`test mode` is enabled, DWR generates test pages (there is a sample screen in Chapter 4) that are useful tools to get to know the DWR functionality.

It is also possible to use JEE access control mechanisms and limit access to DWR itself for specific JEE roles. These are specified in the `web.xml` file. Within DWR, there is also a role-based access control to the methods of remoted Java objects. DWR can also be integrated with Spring Security (also known as Acegi Security), `http://www.acegisecurity.org/`, the official security projects of the Spring Portfolio. The description of Acegi and DWR integration is found on `http://java-x.blogspot.com/2007/08/handling-security-with-ajax-dwr-and.html`.

DWR is also designed so that there is no possibility of an attacker accessing and manipulating DWR core files and changing the security parameters for example.

Minimize Risks

Security is not a trivial issue, and we could spend years in the security field and still leave a lot unfinished. As developers, our job is to make sure that security risks are minimized, and at least realize what might happen if we remote a certain Java method.

A very good example from the DWR website is that if we make a remote call to a method called `appendStringToFile()`, which appends a given string to a predefined file, then a possible attacker can send a large number of requests and fill the file system with nonsense and thus cause an unexpected server downtime. The cost of downtime may be anything from little inconvenience to millions of dollars.

In order to prevent giving accidental access that may cause harm, we have to think of what we want to do and also check the input parameters. Checking input parameters is the most important thing that we as developers can do to make sure accidents do not happen.

In the previous example, if we have remoted the `appendStringToFile()` method, we can do lots of checks on whether the file system is filling, whether it is a string valid for the purpose for which it was meant (such as log entry to a log file), who the requester is, and so on.

Also make sure that `escapeHTML` is used in order to prevent cross-site scripting (XSS) attacks. XSS is something worth knowing about. So please refer to Wikipedia (`http://en.wikipedia.org/wiki/Cross-site_scripting`) for a detailed description.

Summary

This chapter presented an overview of DWR features including JavaScript libraries (`util.js`, `engine.js`, and `gi.js`), security, and Reverse AJAX and on basic operational elements of how DWR works.

In addition to the topics discussed in this chapter, DWR has lots of other useful features that may or may not be relevant to developers. It depends on the application. Topics in this chapter are intended to be high-level overviews, but they will give you a good starting point to learn more from the DWR website (`http://directwebremoting.org/dwr/documentation`) and even from the DWR source code.

Very often, most developers do not need all the features of a technology when they start working on a project. After the project has been going on for some time, we may find out that the solution has matured to include most if not all features of the technology. But that is typically not the initial case and, besides, we have to start somewhere and it is practical to start taking small steps at a time, like toddlers learning to walk.

3
Getting Started

In this chapter, we are going to set up the development environment for the coding work we will do in the following chapters. We will also have a look at supported environments, configuration, testing, and debugging.

As the development environment for the sample code in this book, we have the following components: Eclipse as IDE, Apache Geronimo 2.x.x as the application server, Java 1.5.x as Java runtime, Firefox 2.0.0.x as the client, and Windows as the operating system (Linux would work just as well).

This chapter includes the following sections:

- Supported Browsers and Environments—describes which software components are supported by DWR

- Configuration—presents DWR configuration, including `dwr.xml` and `web.xml` files

- Setting up a development environment—has steps to set up components for development

- Testing and Debugging—describes how to test and debug while developing applications using DWR

- Error Handling—describes how DWR handles error handling, and how it is configured to do it

- Packaging and deployment—shows how to package and deploy DWR applications using Eclipse and Geronimo

Supported Browsers and Environments

As DWR applications are based on Java, the server that runs a DWR application must be a Java server. JDK 1.3 and servlet specification 2.2 are minimum requirements. Almost all Java application servers support DWR applications. Apache Tomcat, Apache Geronimo, WebSphere, Weblogic, and many other servers are supported. In this book, we have used Apache Geronimo.

DWR supports most of the latest browsers:

- Firefox 1.x and later versions are supported.
- Internet Explorer 6.0 and the later versions of Windows are supported (IE Mac is not supported). IE 5.5 may also work, but IE 5.0.2 is not supported.
- Mozilla-based browsers are supported from version 1.7.
- Opera version 7.5.4 and later are supported (only one minor issue reported with strings containing nulls).
- Safari browsers from version 1.2 on OSX are supported.
- Konqueror browser and its latest versions may work, but they are not tested by the DWR team.

In general, most current browsers are supported by DWR, and it is unlikely that browser support is an issue in any current or future development project. Especially, when the project is for **SMB (Small and Medium Businesses)** or an enterprise customer, they probably have a company policy for a preferred browser, and that browser is very likely one of the two major browsers.

Configuration

DWR is configured using XML files, annotations, or Fluent Interface style. Using XML files is the most typical method for DWR configuration, and there are two files: web.xml and dwr.xml. The first one, web.xml, is a must for other configuration methods also. Annotations and fluent-style configurations may be used in place of dwr.xml. This section describes the configuration methods and how to use them.

web.xml

Configuration starts by defining the DWR servlet in the web application's web.xml configuration file. This is, of course, mandatory since DWR would not work without it. A minimum configuration does not have any init parameters, and is shown as follows:

```
<servlet>
  <servlet-name>dwrservlet</servlet-name>
  <servlet-class>org.directwebremoting.servlet.DwrServlet</servlet-
                                                            class>
</servlet>
<servlet-mapping>
  <servlet-name>dwrservlet</servlet-name>
  <url-pattern>/dwrservlet/*</url-pattern>
</servlet-mapping>
```

There are many `init` parameters that are used to configure DWR behavior and the most common parameter is the `debug` parameter. When set to true, the `debug` parameter generates test pages for remoted classes. Test pages could be used to test the DWR functionality and, well, to debug application before moving to production. Never leave the `debug` parameter set to true in a live production environment.

Several `init` parameters are related to security. The following table describes which security parameters are available:

Parameter	Description
`allowGetForSafariButMakeForgeryEasier`	When this parameter is set to true, it enables DWR to work with Safari 1.x browsers. The downside is that security is reduced because GET requests can be forged more easily. The default value is false.
`crossDomainSessionSecurity`	This parameter enables DWR's **CSRF (Cross-Site Request Forgery)** protection, to stop other sites from forging requests using your application's session cookie.
`allowScriptTagRemoting`	Enables script tag remoting. The default value is false, and setting this to true may be a significant security risk. Do not set it to true unless you know what you are doing.
`debug`	Setting this to true enables test and debug pages. The default value is false.
`scriptSessionTimeout`	Refers to the timeout for a script session. The default value is 30 minutes.
`maxCallCount`	Refers to the maximum number of calls in a single batch. The default value is 20. If this number is large, denial-of-service attacks can be done more easily.

Initialization parameters for a DWR servlet also include several parameters for server load protection. The `init` parameters for load protection are listed in the following table:

Parameter	Description
activeReverseAjaxEnabled	When set to true, this enables reverse AJAX support, polling, and Comet. The default value is false.
maxWaitingThreads	The maximum number of threads that wait for requests. The default value is 100.
maxHitsPerSecond	The number of poll requests that we should get per second. The default value is 40.

Other `init` parameters also exist such as `sessionCookieName` and `overridePath`. The DWR web page lists all parameters, including a few undocumented parameters.

dwr.xml

The other XML configuration file for DWR is `dwr.xml`. This file is used to configure remoted Java classes to JavaScript functions, and is the basis of DWR functionality.

The `dwr.xml` file has the following structure:

```
<!DOCTYPE dwr PUBLIC "-//GetAhead Limited//DTD Direct Web Remoting
2.0//EN" "http://getahead.org/dwr/dwr20.dtd">
<dwr>
  <init>
    <creator id="cr1" class="org.mysource.CreatorClass1"/>
    <converter id="co1" class="org.mysource.ConverterClass1"/>
  </init>
  <allow>
    <create creator="new" javascript="ServerClass"/>
    <convert converter="co1" match="org.mysource.MyDataClass"/>
  </allow>
</dwr>
```

The most important entries are within the `allow` element. Without the `allow` element, DWR is of no use since nothing is allowed. Entries within the `init` element are rarely used except when extending DWR. In addition to `init` and `allow` elements there can be a `signatures` element that holds method signatures and is used when our remoted objects have `Collection` parameters (such as `List`). When a method has a `List` parameter, DWR has no way of knowing what types `List` holds. That is why signatures are used to tell DWR that the `List` holds, for example, `String` objects.

Using Creator and Its Attributes

Within the `allow` element there are creators and converters. Creators are used to create JavaScript objects that are used in the browser. The following is the structure of the `create` element:

```
<create creator="..." javascript="..." scope="...">
    <param name="..." value="..."/>
    <auth method="..." role="..."/>
    <exclude method="..."/>
    <include method="..."/>
</create>
```

Only `creator` and `javascript` attributes are mandatory, while others are optional.

The `creator` attribute specifies how DWR creates a Java object. It can be:

- `new`—This uses the Java objects `new` operator. This is very commonly used.
- `none`—It does not create any object. This assumes that the object has already been created by someone else or the method to be called is static.
- `scripted`—It uses a scripting language to create objects. It is useful for example when a remoted Java object is singleton. This requires **BSF** (**Bean Scripting Framework** from Apache http://jakarta.apache.org/bsf/) and any scripting language package, such as BeanShell, in the web application classpath.
- `spring`—It uses Spring Framework to give access to a Java object.
- `jsf`—It enables JSF managed beans to be remoted.
- `struts`—It enables Struts FormBeans as remoted objects.
- `pageflow`—It gives access to Weblogic/Beehive PageFlow objects.

The `javascript` attribute gives the Java object a name that is used in the browser side.

The `scope` element is used to specify where a bean is available. For example, scope can have values: `application`, `request`, `session`, `page`, and `script`. The first four are the same as in servlet development and `script` allows a bean to be tied to an ID in a page rather than an HTTP session cookie. The default scope is page.

The `param` element is used to configure the chosen creator. For example, `new` creator has a parameter called `class`, and its value is a fully qualified class name of the Java class we want to remote. The default constructor is used to create Java objects with the `new` creator.

The `auth` element is used to specify the J2EE role level that is used for access control checking.

Two elements `include` and `exclude` are used to limit access to class methods. One of the elements may be used to limit access. When the `include` element is used DWR assumes that all other methods are restricted except those specified in the `include` element. The `exclude` element on the other hand has the opposite effect and gives access to all methods except to those specified in the `exclude` element. By default, all methods are accessible in the remote object. For example, the following code snippet has two remote objects, `JavaObjectOne` and `JavaObjectTwo`, where the first object allows access to only one method, and the second allows access to all methods except the one specified in the `exclude` element.

```
<create creator="new" javascript="accessorOne">
  <param name="class" value="my.JavaObjectOne"/>
  <include method="getOptionElementsForUser"/>
</create>

<create creator="new" javascript="accessorTwo" scope="session">
  <param name="class" value="my.JavaObjectTwo"/>
  <exclude method="setInternalVariable"/>
</create>
```

Using the Converter Element

The `converter` element is used to specify how method parameters are converted from JavaScript to Java. Converters are not needed if parameters are based on Java primitive types, strings, `java.util.Date` or arrays/collections of mentioned objects.

Converters are needed for custom `JavaBean` and other parameters. For example, for a `JavaBean` such as the following, we would have to specify a Bean converter.

```
package my.package;
public class StockInfo
{
  public void setClosingPrice(double price) { ... }
  public void setVolume(long volume) { ... }
}
```

The Bean converter is provided by DWR, and it converts `JavaBean` objects to JavaScript associative arrays and vice-versa. Entry in `dwr.xml` would be:

```
<convert converter="bean" match="my.package.StockInfo"/>
```

Converters need to be specified manually because it is necessary for DWR to know that it is allowed to touch our code. This feature is good for security since it leaves us the responsibility of giving permissions to certain actions rather than DWR doing something by default that we don't want.

In addition to the Bean converter, there are a few other converters. There is an Object converter, which works directly on object members instead of getters and setters like the Bean converter. Then there are converters for arrays, Java Collections, DOM objects, and enums. Custom converters may also be developed, but it is a rare situation when a custom converter is needed.

Working with Annotations

Annotations were introduced in Java 5, and DWR supports configuration by annotations instead of (or in conjunction with) XML configuration. In order to use annotations, the DWR servlet entry in the `web.xml` file must have all the annotated classes specified in the `classes init` parameter as in the following example.

```
<init-param>
    <param-name>classes</param-name>
    <param-value>
      my.class.StockInfo,
      my.class.OtherInfo
    </param-value>
</init-param>
```

The following is a sample of an annotated class for DWR.

```
@RemoteProxy(name="market")
public class StockMarket
{
    @RemoteMethod
    public double getLatestPrice(String symbol) { ... }
}
```

The annotation `@RemoteProxy` makes a class available for remoting, and the name of its attribute specifies the JavaScript name for the object. All methods that we need for remote access must have the `@RemoteMethod` annotation. Conversions to make custom bean classes are available through `@DataTransferObject` and `@RemoteProperty` annotations.

In comparison, the above `StockInfo` class would have the following entry in the `dwr.xml` configuration.

```
<create creator="new" javascript="market">
  <param name="class" value="my.class.StockMarket"/>
  <include method="getLatestPrice"/>
</create>
```

Using Fluent Configuration with DWR

Fluent configuration style was described by Martin Fowler (`http://www.martinfowler.com/bliki/FluentInterface.html`) a few years ago. The word "Fluent" comes from the ability to "fluently" describe the configuration. Refer to the following example (from the DWR website):

```
public void configure() {
    withConverterType("dog", "com.yourcompany.beans.Dog");
    withCreatorType("ejb", "com.yourcompany.dwr.creator.EJBCreator");
    withCreator("new", "ApartmentDAO")
        .addParam("scope", "session")
        .addParam("class", "com.yourcompany.dao.ApartmentDAO")
        .exclude("saveApartment")
        .withAuth("method", "role");
    withCreator("struts", "DogDAO")
        .addParam("class", "com.yourcompany.dao.DogDAO")
        .include("getDog")
        .include("getColor");
    withConverter("dog", "*.Dog")
        .addParam("name", "value");
    withSignature()
        .addLine("import java.util.List;")
        .addLine("import com.example.Check;")
        .addLine("Check.setLotteryResults(List nos);");
```

Fluent configuration is enabled by programmatic configuration, and in order to use it with DWR, a `customConfigurator` init parameter in the `web.xml` file must point to a class that subclasses the abstract `org.directwebremoting.fluent.FluentConfigurator` class and its `configure` method.

Setting up a Development Environment

development environment that we use in this book is:

1. Java SE 1.5.x
2. DWR 2.0.2
3. Eclipse IDE
4. Apache Geronimo 2.x J2EE application server
5. Firefox browser 2.0.0.x

Development Environment with DWR and Firefox

A development environment for a DWR book is nothing without DWR itself. DWR comes as a JAR file that we add to our web application later. The `dwr.jar` JAR file is less than 500KB in size and it is available at the DWR website, `http://directwebremoting.org/dwr/download`.

The Firefox download site is `http://www.mozilla.com`.

Development Environment with Eclipse

The Eclipse IDE that we use is the recent Eclipse Ganymede release. Eclipse IDE comes in many packages and the one that we use here is Eclipse IDE for Java EE Developers. This package includes tools for developing JEE and web applications, and it has all the prerequisites of the Geronimo Eclipse Plugin that we install here.

The easiest way to install the Geronimo Eclipse Plugin is to let Eclipse **WTP (Web Tools Platform)** to do the download and installation.

- After starting Eclipse, we specify a new server runtime for Geronimo. Go to **New | Other** and the **Select a wizard** dialog opens.

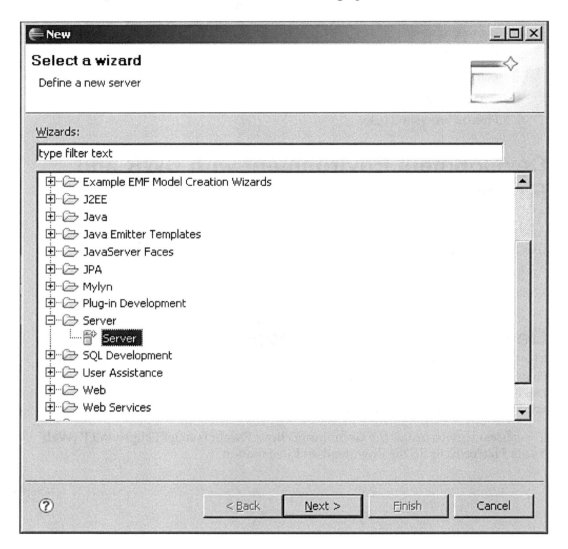

- On clicking **Next**, the **Define a New Server** screen opens.

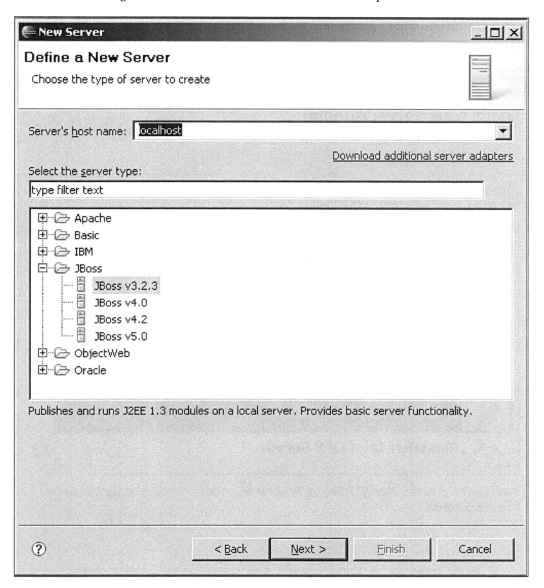

- We set up Geronimo server for Eclipse by clicking on **Download additional server adapters**. Then, the **Install New Adapter** dialog box opens. We select **Geronimo Core Feature** and click on **Next** to continue to accept the license screen. After we accept the license, Eclipse downloads and installs the plugin.

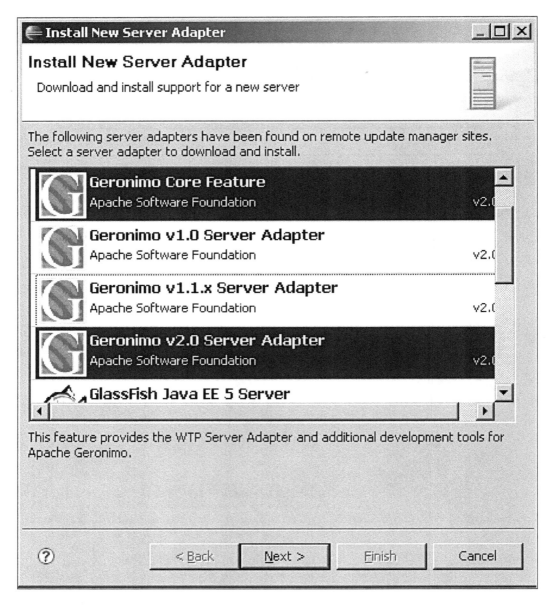

- We repeat the previous step for **Geronimo v2.x Server Adapter**.

Now, the development environment is ready for coding. We have an IDE and a test server, and that's about all we really need.

Apache Geronimo

The Apache Geronimo website is `http://geronimo.apache.org`, and there are downloads for standalone application servers. Even though we have just installed a development environment that includes the Geronimo server runtime, we also need to install standalone Geronimo.

The installation of Geronimo couldn't be simpler! Just download the Geronimo distribution ZIP file (we use the one with Tomcat) and unzip it to some directory. Geronimo is started using the **startup** script in the **bin** directory and stopped using the **shutdown** script.

Testing and Debugging

DWR applications are normal web applications, and so they can be tested and debugged using normal debug tools available in the Eclipse IDE. The Web has information about debugging in Eclipse, for example, the article on the IBM developerWorks site (`http://www.ibm.com/developerworks/opensource/library/os-ecbug/`). Several books about Eclipse and its features are also available.

Another method for debugging is logging. It may sound "old-fashioned", but here is a quote from the book *The Practice of Programming* by Brian W. Kernighan and Rob Pike (this quote is found also from Apache's Log4J website):

> *As personal choice, we tend not to use debuggers beyond getting a stack trace or the value of a variable or two. One reason is that it is easy to get lost in details of complicated data structures and control flow; we find stepping through a program less productive than thinking harder and adding output statements and self-checking code at critical places. Clicking over statements takes longer than scanning the output of judiciously-placed displays. It takes less time to decide where to put print statements than to single-step to the critical section of code, even assuming we know where that is. More important, debugging statements stay with the program; debugging sessions are transient.*

And that basically explains it all.

Testing is done using the Geronimo Server Adapter that we installed in the previous section. We will deploy and test our first DWR sample using the server adapter in the next chapter.

We can also debug in Firefox. Especially if and when we develop our JavaScript functions, it would be good to know that we can also debug JavaScript on the browser. There is a free and open-source tool called Firebug (http://www.getfirebug.com/) that provides several extremely useful features such as inspection of HTML (refer to the following screenshot where the page logo is highlighted), editing JavaScript on a live page, editing CSS, and so on.

It is also possible to debug without Firebug by using JavaScript alert boxes and modification of the browser status line. But Firebug and Firefox make our web development so much easier that it would be cumbersome to work otherwise.

Error Handling

DWR has a concept called handlers for error handling and exception handling on the browser side. Four different handlers have been specified by DWR:

- **errorHandler** is used when DWR knows for certain that something is broken, for example, when the application server has been stopped.

- **warningHandler** is used by DWR when something is wrong, but DWR cannot automatically define the severity of that "something". This is useful during development while debugging an application.

- **exceptionHandler** is used to catch exceptions that are thrown by the server side code. Since we are likely to want to know about exceptions, errorHandler is used if no exceptionHandler is defined.

- **textHtmlHandler** handles non-JavaScript responses. Usually, this happens when the server session has expired, and the server presents a login screen or info screen about the expired session.

Handlers are set in JavaScript code on the client using a function in the engine.js package:

```
dwr.engine.setErrorHandler(handlerFunction);
```

Exceptions are handled by exceptionHandler or errorHandler. By default, when an exception happens, DWR does not include any information about the exception in the error message. For example, an exception object may look like this:

```
{
  javaClassName:'java.lang.Throwable',
  message:'Error'
}
```

"Error" says nothing about what might be wrong, except that something is clearly wrong. More detailed exceptions are enabled by adding the following line to dwr.xml.

```
<convert match="java.lang.Exception" converter="exception"/>
```

The Exception converter enables understandable error messages:

```
{
  javaClassName:'org.xml.sax.SAXParseException',
  lineNumber:42,
  publicId:'somePublicId',
  message:'Missing >'
}
```

Further, enabling stacktraces using the line `<convert match="java.lang. StackTraceElement" converter="bean"/>` in dwr.xml allows easier development work where we can see errors as they occur and go directly to the debugging mode.

Session expiry is handled by textHtmlHandler, and it is used like this:

```
dwr.engine.setTextHtmlHandler(function() {
  window.alert("Your session has expired, please login again." );
  document.location = '/mycontext/login';
});
```

When DWR receives a response from the server that includes unexpected HTML, the cause for which is very likely because the session has expired, and the application server returns information page about the session expiry or the actual login page, the Handler function receives an object that contains HTTP status code, response text, and content MIME type from DWR.

Packaging and Deployment

In this section, we package and deploy a simple web application to the standalone Geronimo application server. The Geronimo console and command-line tools are used here to deploy the application, but in the further chapters, we use the Geronimo test environment within the Eclipse IDE.

- This simple **HelloWorldServlet** has been created as a sample for packaging and deployment.

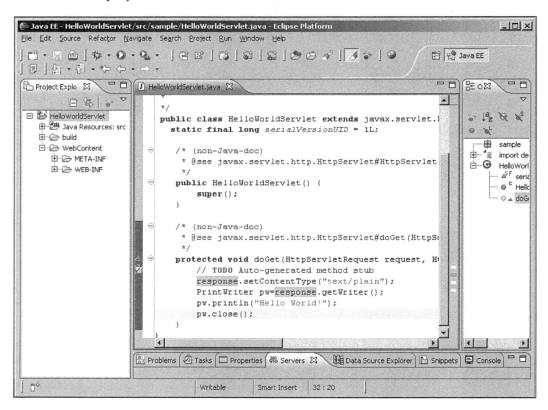

Packaging is easy because of built-in Eclipse tools.

- We select the project name and right-click to get the context menu; under the **Export** menu item, we find the **WAR** option.

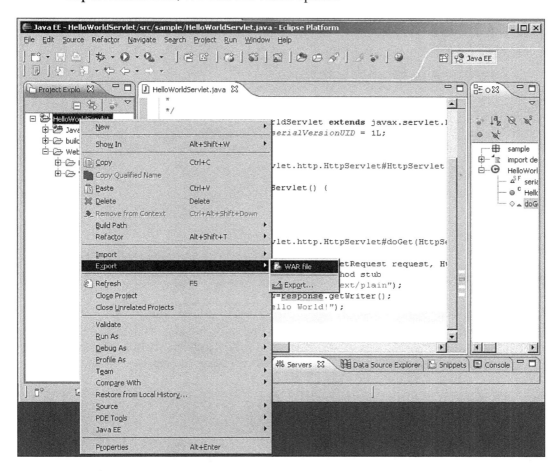

- After we click the **WAR** option, a **WAR Export** dialog opens where we choose the **Destination** and a name for the WAR file: **d:\temp\HelloWorldServlet.war**.

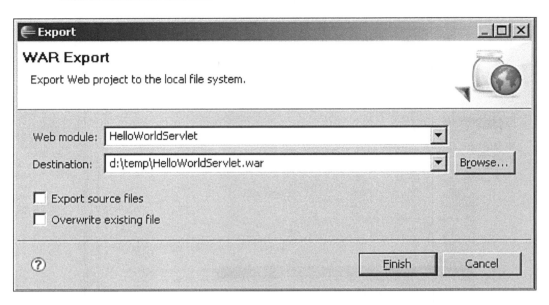

- For the deployment, we have installed a standalone Geronimo application server. Run Geronimo using the **startup** script file (and remember to set the JAVA_HOME environment variable). The following screenshot displays typical output when starting the Geronimo server using the **startup** script.

```
Geronimo                                                                  _ □ ×
   8443 0.0.0.0    Tomcat Connector HTTPS BIO HTTPS
   9999 0.0.0.0    JMX Remoting Connector
  61613 0.0.0.0    ActiveMQ Transport Connector
  61616 0.0.0.0    ActiveMQ Transport Connector

Started Application Modules:
  EAR: org.apache.geronimo.configs/webconsole-tomcat/2.0.2/car
  JAR: org.apache.geronimo.configs/mejb/2.0.2/car
  RAR: org.apache.geronimo.configs/activemq-ra/2.0.2/car
  RAR: org.apache.geronimo.configs/system-database/2.0.2/car
  WAR: org.apache.geronimo.configs/dojo-tomcat/2.0.2/car
  WAR: org.apache.geronimo.configs/remote-deploy-tomcat/2.0.2/car
  WAR: org.apache.geronimo.configs/welcome-tomcat/2.0.2/car
  WAR: sample/HelloWorldServlet/1.0/car

Web Applications:
  /
  /HelloWorldServlet
  /console
  /console-standard
  /dojo
  /remote-deploy

Geronimo Application Server started
```

Deployment Using the Administration Console

Deployment can be done using the Geronimo Administration Console.

1. After starting the Geronimo server, open Geronimo web console. The default
    location is `http://127.0.0.1:8080/console`. The default administrator
    user name is **system**, and the password is **manager**. After login to the system,
    we will see the **Geronimo Administration Console**. On the left side, there
    is a menu for administrative tasks, and on the right side there are links to
    common tasks, documentation, and other resources.

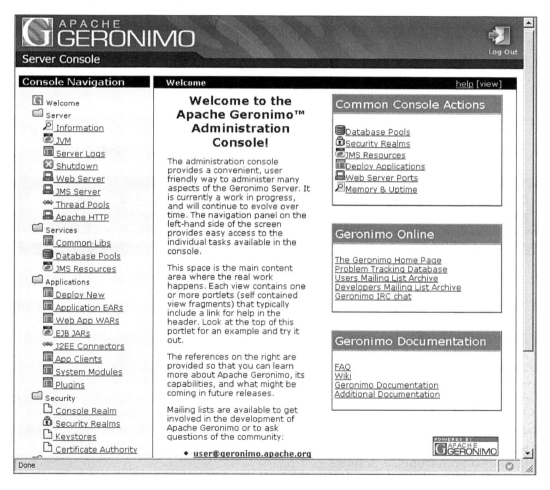

2. Installation is a straightforward task. We select **Deploy Applications** present in the **Common Console Actions** box or **Deploy New Application** present on the left in **Console Navigation**. The following screen opens where we specify the `HelloWorldServlet.war` file.

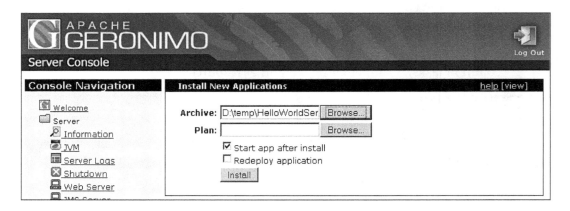

3. After pressing **Install**, Geronimo displays the status of the operation.

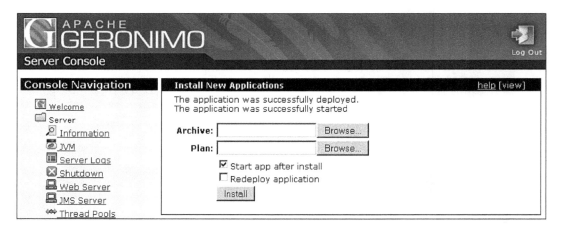

Now that the application has been installed, we can test it. There are two things we need to know: context path and servlet mapping. We specified the servlet mapping during development, and we get it from the `web.xml` file; it is **HelloWorld**. We get the context path from Geronimo.

4. The Web App WAR's link in the **Console Navigation** opens an **Installed Web Applications** screen, and there we see a list of applications and in the URL column there is the context path.

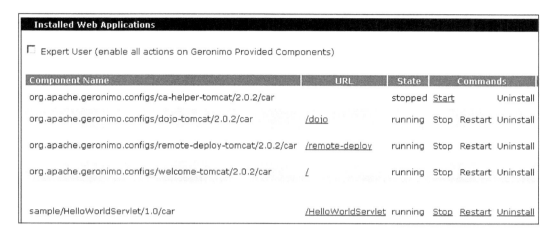

5. Now that we have context path and servlet mapping, we open our servlet in a browser: `http://127.0.0.1:8080/HelloWorldServlet/HelloWorld` and we are able to see the world famous message.

Uninstalling, stopping, and restarting of applications are done via the **Installed Web Applications** screen.

The Administration console is very useful especially when we start to perform development work or while occasionally testing some applications in Geronimo. However, during development, it is better to use a command-line-based deployer tool.

Deployment Using the Deployer Tool

The Deployer tool is a command-line tool that is used primarily to install and uninstall applications in Geronimo. Tool is located in the **bin** directory and it is either `deploy.bat` or `deploy.sh` depending on the operating system.

The tool syntax is:

```
deploy.[bat|sh] [general options] command [command options]
```

To install a new WAR file, we use the `deploy` command:

```
deploy -user system -password manager deploy d:\temp\
HelloWorldServlet.war
```

We get the following confirmation screen about successful installation:

```
D:\apps\geronimo-tomcat6-jee5-2.0.2\bin>deploy --user system --password manager
deploy d:\temp\HelloWorldServlet.war
Using GERONIMO_BASE:    D:\apps\geronimo-tomcat6-jee5-2.0.2
Using GERONIMO_HOME:    D:\apps\geronimo-tomcat6-jee5-2.0.2
Using GERONIMO_TMPDIR: var\temp
Using JRE_HOME:         d:\apps\jdk1.5.0_14\jre
    Deployed sample/HelloWorldServlet/1.0/car @ /HelloWorldServlet
```

Note that we get more information when we install using the command-line tool than when installing it by using the administration console. We see the module name and also the context root from the prompt. The module name is important because that is used to uninstall the application. The uninstall command is:

```
deploy -user system -password manager undeploy sample/
HelloWorldServlet/1.0/car
```

Another important command is `list modules`, which shows all the installed modules currently running in the application server. All other commands for the `deploy` command are found in the Geronimo documentation.

The deployer tool is probably the most useful way to do deployment. It allows automation of the deployment process, and we can minimize manual errors. Not to mention, it is much, much faster to let the script do the deployment rather than manually installing using the administration console.

Deployment Using Hot Deployment

Hot deployment is the easiest method of installation. Here, we just copy our sample WAR file to Geronimo's **deploy** directory, and Geronimo does the rest. We can verify the installation using the `list modules` command of the deployer tool.

Uninstallation is also straightforward. We delete the WAR file from the `deploy` directory and Geronimo will uninstall the application.

Hot deployment is useful for quick and possibly dirty installations of applications. In real life, it may probably be better to use the deployer command-line tool because of scripting, and the automation that results from scripting the deployment process.

Summary

Now, we have set up our development environment and also taken a look at supported environments, testing, debugging, packaging, and deployment. We have also covered configuration of DWR. So everything is in good shape to start working with DWR.

The rest of the book will concentrate on the real code, and we will see DWR features that were introduced in this and the earlier chapters.

4
User Interface: Basic Elements

In this chapter, we will get to the actual hands-on work. We will develop samples based on DWR, which show how to dynamically change the common user interface elements such as tables and lists as well as field completion. We also make a dynamic user interface skeleton for our samples that will hold all the samples in this book.

The section on dynamic user interfaces shows how to get started with a DWR application, and it presents a user interface skeleton that will be used to hold the tables and lists sample, and the field completion (aka. autosuggest/autocomplete) sample. Samples in the following chapter will use the same user interface skeleton, with the exception of the sample applications in Chapter 7.

The following are the sections in this chapter:

- Creating a Dynamic User Interface — starts with creating a web project and a basis for samples mentioned in this chapter
- Implementing Tables and Lists — shows us how to use DWR with them
- Implementing Field Completion — has a sample for typical field completion

Creating a Dynamic User Interface

The idea behind a dynamic user interface is to have a common "framework" for all samples. We will create a new web application and then add new features to the application as we go on. The user interface will look something like the following figure:

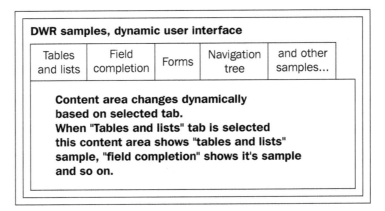

The user interface has three main areas: the title/logo that is static, the tabs that are dynamic, and the content area that shows the actual content.

The idea behind this implementation is to use DWR functionality to generate tabs and to get content for the tab pages. The tabbed user interface is created using a CSS template from the Dynamic Drive CSS Library (`http://dynamicdrive.com/style/csslibrary/item/css-tabs-menu`). Tabs are read from a properties file, so it is possible to dynamically add new tabs to the web page. The following screenshot shows the user interface.

The following sequence diagram shows the application flow from the logical perspective. Because of the built-in DWR features we don't need to worry very much about how asynchronous AJAX "stuff" works. This is, of course, a Good Thing.

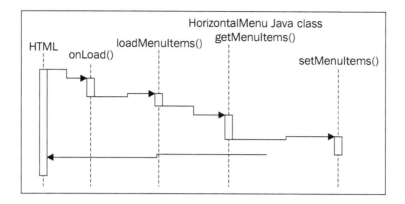

Now we will develop the application using the Eclipse IDE and the Geronimo test environment that we set up in the previous chapter.

Creating a New Web Project

1. First, we will create a new web project. Using the Eclipse IDE we do the following: select the menu **File | New | Dynamic Web Project**.

2. This opens the **New Dynamic Web Project** dialog; enter the project name **DWREasyAjax** and click **Next**, and accept the defaults on all the pages till the last page, where **Geronimo Deployment Plan** is created as shown in the following screenshot:

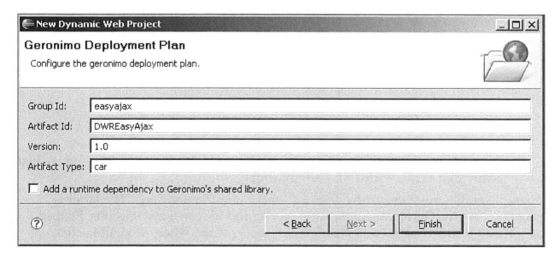

3. Enter **easyajax** as **Group Id** and **DWREasyAjax** as **Artifact Id**. On clicking **Finish**, Eclipse creates a new web project. The following screen shot shows the generated project and the directory hierarchy.

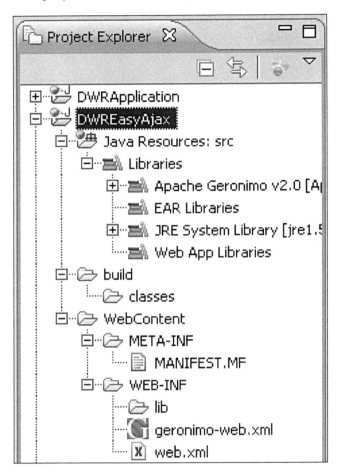

4. Before starting to do anything else, we need to copy DWR to our web application. All DWR functionality is present in the dwr.jar file, and we just copy that to the **WEB-INF | lib** directory.

A couple of files are noteworthy: web.xml and geronimo-web.xml. The latter is generated for the Geronimo application server, and we can leave it as it is. Eclipse has an editor to show the contents of geronimo-web.xml when we double-click the file.

```
G  Geronimo Deployment Plan Editor  ✕

Web Deployment Plan General Configuration

  ▼ General
    Edit the common deployment settings.

    Group Id:        easyajax

    Artifact Id:     DWREasyAjax

    Version:         1.0

    Artifact Type:   car

    ☐  Inverse classloading
    ☐  Supress default environment
    ☐  Add a runtime dependency to Geronimo's shared library.

    Context Root:    /DWREasyAjax
```

Configuring the Web Application

The context root is worth noting (visible in the screenshot above). We will need it when we test the application.

The other XML file, web.xml, is very important as we all know. This XML will hold the DWR servlet definition and other possible initialization parameters. The following code shows the full contents of the web.xml file that we will use:

```
<?xml version="1.0" encoding="UTF-8"?>
<web-app xmlns:xsi="http://www.w3.org/2001/XMLSchema-instance"
  xmlns="http://java.sun.com/xml/ns/javaee"
  xmlns:web="http://java.sun.com/xml/ns/javaee/web-app_2_5.xsd"
  xsi:schemaLocation="http://java.sun.com/xml/ns/javaee http://java.
sun.com/xml/ns/javaee/web-app_2_5.xsd"
  id="WebApp_ID" version="2.5">
  <display-name>DWREasyAjax</display-name>
  <servlet>
    <display-name>DWR Servlet</display-name>
    <servlet-name>dwr-invoker</servlet-name>
    <servlet-class>
      org.directwebremoting.servlet.DwrServlet
```

```
      </servlet-class>
      <init-param>
        <param-name>debug</param-name>
        <param-value>true</param-value>
      </init-param>
    </servlet>

    <servlet-mapping>
      <servlet-name>dwr-invoker</servlet-name>
      <url-pattern>/dwr/*</url-pattern>
    </servlet-mapping>

    <welcome-file-list>
      <welcome-file>index.html</welcome-file>
      <welcome-file>index.htm</welcome-file>
      <welcome-file>index.jsp</welcome-file>
      <welcome-file>default.html</welcome-file>
      <welcome-file>default.htm</welcome-file>
      <welcome-file>default.jsp</welcome-file>
    </welcome-file-list>
  </web-app>
```

We have already seen the `servlet` definition in Chapter 3, in the section on configuration. We use the same `debug-init` parameter here. Servlet mapping is the commonly used `/dwr/*`.

We remember that DWR cannot function without the `dwr.xml` configuration file. So we need to create the configuration file. We use Eclipse to create a new XML file in the **WEB-INF** directory. The following is required for the user interface skeleton. It already includes the `allow`-element for our DWR based menu.

```
<?xml version="1.0" encoding="UTF-8"?>
<!DOCTYPE dwr PUBLIC
    "-//GetAhead Limited//DTD Direct Web Remoting 2.0//EN"
    "http://getahead.org/dwr/dwr20.dtd">
<dwr>
  <allow>
    <create creator="new" javascript="HorizontalMenu">
      <param name="class" value="samples.HorizontalMenu" />
    </create>
  </allow>
</dwr>
```

In the `allow` element, there is a creator for the horizontal menu Java class that we are going to implement here. The creator that we use here is the `new` creator, which means that DWR will use an empty constructor to create Java objects for clients. The parameter named `class` holds the fully qualified class name.

Developing the Web Application

Since we have already defined the name of the Java class that will be used for creating the menu, the next thing we do is implement it. The idea behind the HorizontalMenu class is that it is used to read a properties file that holds the menus that are going to be on the web page.

We add properties to a file named dwrapplication.properties, and we create it in the same samples-package as the HorizontalMenu-class. The properties file for the menu items is as follows:

```
menu.1=Tables and lists,TablesAndLists
menu.2=Field completion,FieldCompletion
```

The syntax for the menu property is that it contains two elements separated by a comma. The first element is the name of the menu item. This is visible to user. The second is the name of HTML template file that will hold the page content of the menu item.

The class contains just one method, which is used from JavaScript and via DWR to retrieve the menu items. The full class implementation is shown here:

```java
package samples;

import java.io.IOException;
import java.io.InputStream;
import java.util.List;
import java.util.Properties;
import java.util.Vector;

public class HorizontalMenu {
    public HorizontalMenu() {
    }

    public List<String> getMenuItems() throws IOException {
        List<String> menuItems = new Vector<String>();
        InputStream is = this.getClass().getClassLoader().
getResourceAsStream(
                "samples/dwrapplication.properties");
        Properties appProps = new Properties();
        appProps.load(is);
        is.close();
        for (int menuCount = 1; true; menuCount++) {
            String menuItem = appProps.getProperty("menu." + menuCount);
            if (menuItem == null) {
                break;
            }
            menuItems.add(menuItem);
        }
        return menuItems;
    }
}
```

The implementation is straightforward. The `getMenuItems()` method loads properties using the `ClassLoader.getResourceAsStream()` method, which searches the class path for the specified resource. Then, after loading properties, a `for` loop is used to loop through menu items and then a `List` of `String-objects` is returned to the client. The client is the JavaScript callback function that we will see later. DWR automatically converts the `List` of `String` objects to JavaScript arrays, so we don't have to worry about that.

Testing the Web Application

We haven't completed any client-side code now, but let's test the code anyway. Testing uses the Geronimo test environment.

1. The **Project** context menu has the **Run As** menu that we use to test the application as shown in the following screenshot:

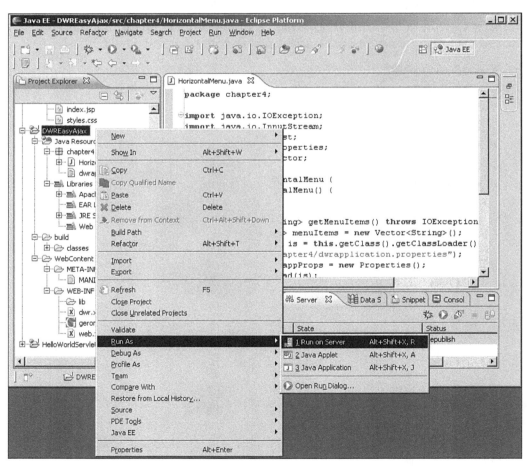

2. **Run on Server** opens a wizard to define a new server runtime. The following screenshot shows that the Geronimo test environment has already been set up, and we just click **Finish** to run the application. If the test environment is not set up, we can manually define a new one in this dialog:

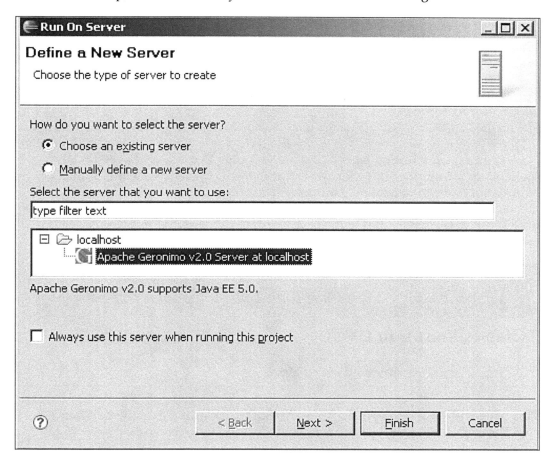

3. After we click **Finish**, Eclipse starts the Geronimo test environment and our application with it. When the server starts, the **Console** tab in Eclipse informs us that it's been started.

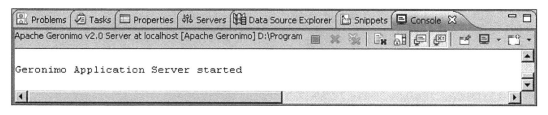

The **Servers** tab shows that the server is started and all the code has been synchronized, that is, the code is the most recent (Synchronization happens whenever we save changes on some deployed file.) The **Servers** tab also has a list of deployed applications under the server. Just the one application that we are testing here is visible in the **Servers** tab.

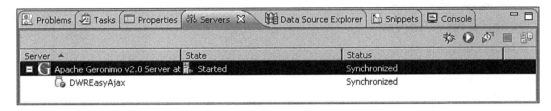

Now comes the interesting part — what are we going to test if we haven't really implemented anything? If we take a look at the web.xml file, we will find that we have defined one initialization parameter. The Debug parameter is true, which means that DWR generates test pages for our remoted Java classes. We just point the browser (Firefox in our case) to the URL http://127.0.0.1:8080/DWREasyAjax/dwr and the following page opens up:

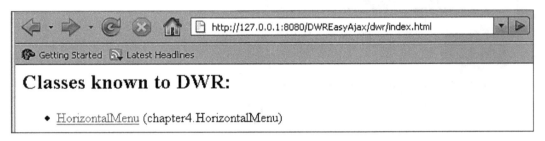

This page will show a list of all the classes that we allow to be remoted. When we click the class name, a test page opens as in the following screenshot:

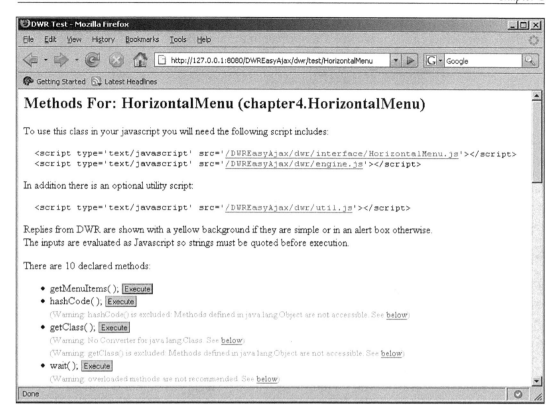

This is an interesting page. We see all the allowed methods, in this case, all public class methods since we didn't specifically include or exclude anything. The most important ones are the script elements, which we need to include in our HTML pages. DWR does not automatically know what we want in our web pages, so we must add the script includes in each page where we are using DWR and a remoted functionality.

Then there is the possibility of testing remoted methods. When we test our own method, getMenuItems(), we see a response in an alert box:

The array in the alert box in the screenshot is the JavaScript array that DWR returns from our method.

Developing Web Pages

The next step is to add the web pages. Note that we can leave the test environment running. Whenever we change the application code, it is automatically published to test the environment, so we don't need to stop and start the server each time we make some changes and want to test the application.

The CSS style sheet is from the Dynamic Drive CSS Library. The file is named styles.css, and it is in the **WebContent** directory in Eclipse IDE. The CSS code is as shown:

```
/*URL: http://www.dynamicdrive.com/style/ */

.basictab{
padding: 3px 0;
margin-left: 0;
font: bold 12px Verdana;
border-bottom: 1px solid gray;
list-style-type: none;
text-align: left; /*set to left, center, or right to align the menu as
desired*/
}

.basictab li{
display: inline;
margin: 0;
}
```

```
.basictab li a{
text-decoration: none;
padding: 3px 7px;
margin-right: 3px;
border: 1px solid gray;
border-bottom: none;
background-color: #f6ffd5;
color: #2d2b2b;
}

.basictab li a:visited{
color: #2d2b2b;
}

.basictab li a:hover{
background-color: #DBFF6C;
color: black;
}

.basictab li a:active{
color: black;
}

.basictab li.selected a{ /*selected tab effect*/
position: relative;
top: 1px;
padding-top: 4px;
background-color: #DBFF6C;
color: black;
}
```

This CSS is shown for the sake of completion, and we will not go into details of CSS style sheets. It is sufficient to say that CSS provides an excellent method to create websites with good presentation.

The next step is the actual web page. We create an index.jsp page, in the **WebContent** directory, which will have the menu and also the JavaScript functions for our samples. It should be noted that although all JavaScript code is added to a single JSP page here in this sample, in "real" projects it would probably be more useful to create a separate file for JavaScript functions and include the JavaScript file in the HTML/JSP page using a code snippet such as this:

```
<script type="text/javascript" src="myjavascriptcode/
HorizontalMenu.js"/>.
```

We will add JavaScript functions later for each sample. The following is the JSP code that shows the menu using the remoted `HorizontalMenu` class.

```
<%@ page language="java" contentType="text/html; charset=ISO-8859-1"
    pageEncoding="ISO-8859-1"%>
<!DOCTYPE html PUBLIC "-//W3C//DTD HTML 4.01 Transitional//EN"
"http://www.w3.org/TR/html4/loose.dtd">
<html>
<head>
<meta http-equiv="Content-Type" content="text/html; charset=ISO-8859-
 1">
<link href="styles.css" rel="stylesheet" type="text/css"/>
<script type='text/javascript' src='/DWREasyAjax/dwr/engine.js'></
script>
<script type='text/javascript' src='/DWREasyAjax/dwr/util.js'></
script>
<script type='text/javascript' src='/DWREasyAjax/dwr/interface/
HorizontalMenu.js'></script>
<title>DWR samples</title>
<script type="text/javascript">

function loadMenuItems()
{
  HorizontalMenu.getMenuItems(setMenuItems);
}

function getContent(contentId)
{
  AppContent.getContent(contentId,setContent);
}

function menuItemFormatter(item)
{
  elements=item.split(',');
  return '<li><a href="#" onclick="getContent(\''+elements[1]+'\
');return false;">'+elements[0]+'</a></li>';
}

function setMenuItems(menuItems)
{
  menu=dwr.util.byId("dwrMenu");
  menuItemsHtml='';
  for(var i=0;i<menuItems.length;i++)
  {
    menuItemsHtml=menuItemsHtml+menuItemFormatter(menuItems[i]);
  }
  menu.innerHTML=menuItemsHtml;
}

function setContent(htmlArray)
{
```

```
     var contentFunctions='';
     var scriptToBeEvaled='';
     var contentHtml='';
     for(var i=0;i<htmlArray.length;i++)
     {
       var html=htmlArray[i];
       if(html.toLowerCase().indexOf('<script')>-1)
       {
         if(html.indexOf('TO BE EVALED')>-1)
         {
           scriptToBeEvaled=html.substring(html.indexOf('>')+1,
                                             html.indexOf('</'));
         }
         else
         {
           eval(html.substring(html.indexOf('>')+1,html.indexOf('</')));
           contentFunctions+=html;
         }
       }
       else
       {
         contentHtml+=html;
       }
     }

   contentScriptArea=dwr.util.byId("contentAreaFunctions");
   contentScriptArea.innerHTML=contentFunctions;
   contentArea=dwr.util.byId("contentArea");
   contentArea.innerHTML=contentHtml;
   if(scriptToBeEvaled!='')
   {
     eval(scriptToBeEvaled);
   }
}
</script>
</head>
<body onload="loadMenuItems()">
<h1>DWR Easy Java Ajax Applications</h1>
<ul class="basictab" id="dwrMenu">
</ul>
<div id="contentAreaFunctions">
</div>
<div id="contentArea">
</div>
</body>
</html>
```

This JSP is our user interface. The HTML is just normal HTML with a head element and a body element. The head includes reference to a style sheet and to DWR JavaScript files, engine.js, util.js, and our own HorizontalMenu.js. The util.js file is optional, but as it contains very useful functions, it could be included in all the web pages where we use the functions in util.js.

The body element has a contentArea place holder for the content pages just below the menu. It also contains the content area for JavaScript functions for a particular content.The body element onload-event executes the loadMenuItems() function when the page is loaded. The loadMenuItems() function calls the remoted method of the HorizontalMenu Java class. The parameter of the HorizontalMenu.getMenuItems() JavaScript function is the callback function that is called by DWR when the Java method has been executed and it returns menu items.

The setMenuItems() function is a callback function for the loadMenuItems() function mentioned in the previous paragraph. While loading menu items, the Horizontal.getMenuItems() remoted method returns menu items as a List of Strings as a parameter to the setMenuItems() function. The menu items are formatted using the menuItemFormatter() helper function.

The menuItemFormatter() function creates li elements of menu texts. Menus are formatted as links, (a href) and they have an onclick event that has a function call to the getContent-function, which in turn calls the AppContent.getContent() function.

The AppContent is a remoted Java class, which we haven't implemented yet, and its purpose is to read the HTML from a file based on the menu item that the user clicked. Implementation of AppContent and the content pages are described in the next section.

The setContent() function sets the HTML content to the content area and also evaluates JavaScript options that are within the content to be inserted in the content area (this is not used very much, but it is there for those who need it).

Our dynamic user interface looks like this:

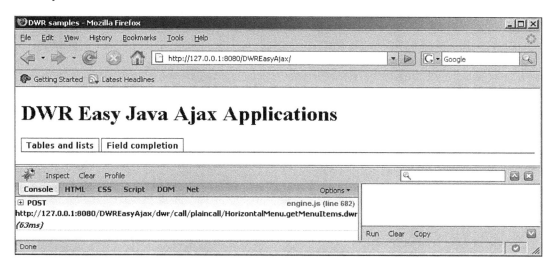

Note the Firebug window at the bottom of the browser screen. The Firebug console in the screenshot shows one POST request to our `HorizontalMenu.getMenuItems()` method. Other Firebug features are extremely useful during development work, and we find it useful that Firebug has been enabled throughout the development work.

Callback Functions

We saw our first callback function as a parameter in the `HorizontalMenu.getMen uItems(setMenuItems)` function, and since callbacks are an important concept in DWR, it would be good to discuss a little more about them now that we have seen their first usage.

Callbacks are used to operate on the data that was returned from a remoted method. As DWR and AJAX are asynchronous, typical return values in **RPCs** (**Remote Procedure Calls**), as in Java calls, do not work. DWR hides the details of calling the callback functions and handles everything internally from the moment we return a value from the remoted Java method to receiving the returned value to the callback function.

Two methods are recommended while using callback functions.

We have already seen the first method in the `HorizontalMenu.getMenuItems` (`setMenuItems`) function call. Remember that there are no parameters in the `getMenuItems()` Java method, but in the JavaScript call, we added the callback function name at the end of the parameter list. If the Java method has parameters, then the JavaScript call is similar to `CountryDB.getCountries(selectedLett ers,setCountryRows)`, where `selectedLetters` is the input parameter for the Java method and `setCountryRows` is the name of the callback function (we see the implementation later on).

The second method to use callbacks is a meta-data object in the remote JavaScript call. An example (a full implementation is shown later in this chapter) is shown here:

```
CountryDB.saveCountryNotes(ccode,newNotes, {
  callback:function(newNotes)
  {
    //function body here
  }
});
```

Here, the function is anonymous and its implementation is included in the JavaScript call to the remoted Java method. One advantage here is that it is easy to read the code, and the the code is executed immediately after we get the return value from the Java method. The other advantage is that we can add extra options to the call.

Extra options include timeout and error handler as shown in the following example:

```
CountryDB.saveCountryNotes(ccode,newNotes, {
  callback:function(newNotes)
  {
    //function body here
  },
  timeout:10000,
  errorHandler:function(errorMsg) { alert(errorMsg);}
});
```

It is also possible to add a callback function to those Java methods that do not return a value. Adding a callback to methods with no return values would be useful in getting a notification when a remote call has been completed.

Afterword

Our first sample is ready, and it is also the basis for the following samples. We also looked at how applications are tested in the Eclipse environment.

Using DWR, we can look at JavaScript code on the browser and Java code on the server as one. It may take a while to get used to it, but it will change the way we develop web applications. Logically, there is no longer a client and a server but just a single run time platform that happens to be physically separate. But in practice, of course, applications using DWR, JavaScript on the client and Java in the server, are using the typical client-server interaction. This should be remembered when writing applications in the logically single run-time platform.

Implementing Tables and Lists

The first actual sample is very common in applications: tables and lists. In this sample, the table is populated using the DWR utility functions, and a remoted Java class. The sample code also shows how DWR is used to do inline table editing. When a table cell is double-clicked, an edit box opens, and it is used to save new cell data.

The sample will have country data in a CSV file: country **Name**, **Long Name**, two-letter **Code**, **Capital**, and user-defined **Notes**. The user interface for the table sample appears as shown in the following screenshot:

DWR Easy Java Ajax Applications

| Tables and lists | Field completion |

Countries

Show countries starting with [F ▼]
Doubleclick "Notes"-cell to add notes to country.

Name	Long name	Code	Capital	Notes
Fiji	Republic of theFiji Islands	FJ	Suva	
Finland	Republic of Finland	FI	Helsinki	
France	French Republic	FR	Paris	

Server Code for Tables and Lists

The first thing to do is to get the country data. Country data is in a CSV file (named countries.csv and located in the samples Java package). The following is an excerpt of the content of the CSV file (data is from http://www.state.gov).

```
Short-form name,Long-form name,FIPS Code,Capital

Afghanistan,Islamic Republic of Afghanistan,AF,Kabul

Albania,Republic of Albania,AL,Tirana

Algeria,People's Democratic Republic of Algeria,AG,Algiers

Andorra,Principality of Andorra,AN,Andorra la Vella

Angola,Republic of Angola,AO,Luanda

Antigua and Barbuda,(no long-form name),AC,Saint John's

Argentina,Argentine Republic,AR,Buenos Aires

Armenia,Republic of Armenia,AM,Yerevan

...
```

The CSV file is read each time a client requests country data. Although this is not very efficient, it is good enough here. Other alternatives include an in-memory cache or a real database such as Apache Derby or IBM DB2. As an example, we have created a CountryDB class that is used to read and write the country CSV. We also have another class, DBUtils, which has some helper methods. The DBUtils code is as follows:

```
package samples;

import java.io.BufferedReader;
import java.io.File;
import java.io.FileReader;
import java.io.FileWriter;
import java.io.IOException;
import java.io.InputStream;
```

```java
import java.io.InputStreamReader;
import java.io.PrintWriter;
import java.util.List;
import java.util.Vector;

public class DBUtils {

    private String fileName=null;
    public void initFileDB(String fileName)
    {
        this.fileName=fileName;
        // copy csv file to bin-directory, for easy
        // file access
        File countriesFile = new File(fileName);
        if (!countriesFile.exists()) {
            try {
                List<String> countries = getCSVStrings(null);
                PrintWriter pw;
                pw = new PrintWriter(new FileWriter(countriesFile));
                for (String country : countries) {
                    pw.println(country);
                }
                pw.close();
            } catch (IOException e) {
                e.printStackTrace();
            }
        }

    }

    protected List<String> getCSVStrings(String letter) {
        List<String> csvData = new Vector<String>();
        try {
            File csvFile = new File(fileName);
            BufferedReader br = null;
            if(csvFile.exists())
            {
                br=new BufferedReader(new FileReader(csvFile));
            }
            else
            {
                InputStream is = this.getClass().getClassLoader()
                .getResourceAsStream("samples/"+fileName);
                br=new BufferedReader(new InputStreamReader(is));
                br.readLine();
            }

            for (String line = br.readLine(); line != null; line =
br.readLine()) {
                if (letter == null
```

```
                        || (letter != null && line.startsWith(letter))) {
                csvData.add(line);
            }
        }
        br.close();
    } catch (IOException ioe) {
        ioe.printStackTrace();
    }
    return csvData;
    }
}
```

The DBUtils class is a straightforward utility class that returns CSV content as a List of Strings. It also copies the original CSV file to the runtime directory of any application server we might be running. This may not be the best practice, but it makes it easier to manipulate the CSV file, and we always have the original CSV file untouched if and when we need to go back to the original version.

The code for CountryDB is given here:

```java
package samples;

import java.io.FileWriter;
import java.io.IOException;
import java.io.PrintWriter;
import java.util.Arrays;
import java.util.List;
import java.util.Vector;

public class CountryDB {

    private DBUtils dbUtils = new DBUtils();
    private String fileName = "countries.csv";

    public CountryDB() {
    dbUtils.initFileDB(fileName);
    }

    public String[] getCountryData(String ccode) {
        List<String> countries = dbUtils.getCSVStrings(null);
        for (String country : countries) {
            if (country.indexOf("," + ccode + ",") > -1) {
                return country.split(",");
            }
        }
        return new String[0];
    }
```

```
public List<List<String>> getCountries(String startLetter) {

    List<List<String>> allCountryData = new Vector<List<String>>();
    List<String> countryData = dbUtils.getCSVStrings(startLetter);
    for (String country : countryData) {
        String[] data = country.split(",");
        allCountryData.add(Arrays.asList(data));
    }
    return allCountryData;
}

public String[] saveCountryNotes(String ccode, String notes) {
    List<String> countries = dbUtils.getCSVStrings(null);
    try {
        PrintWriter pw = new PrintWriter(new FileWriter(fileName));
        for (String country : countries) {
            if (country.indexOf("," + ccode + ",") > -1) {
                if (country.split(",").length == 4) {
                    // no existing notes
                    country = country + "," + notes;
                } else {
                    if (notes.length() == 0) {
                        country = country.substring(0, country
                                .lastIndexOf(","));
                    } else {
                        country = country.substring(0, country
                                .lastIndexOf(","))
                                + "," + notes;
                    }

                }
            }
            pw.println(country);
        }
        pw.close();
    } catch (IOException ioe) {
        ioe.printStackTrace();
    }
    String[] rv = new String[2];
    rv[0] = ccode;
    rv[1] = notes;
    return rv;
}
}
```

The CountryDB class is a remoted class. The getCountryData() method returns country data as an array of strings based on the country code. The getCountries() method returns all the countries that start with the specified parameter, and saveCountryNotes() saves user added notes to the country specified by the country code.

In order to use CountryDB, the following script element must be added to the index.jsp file together with other JavaScript elements.

```
<script type='text/javascript' src='/DWREasyAjax/dwr/interface/
CountryDB.js'></script>
```

There is one other Java class that we need to create and remote. That is the AppContent class that was already present in the JavaScript functions of the home page. The AppContent class is responsible for reading the content of the HTML file and parses the possible JavaScript function out of it, so it can become usable by the existing JavaScript functions in index.jsp file.

```
package samples;

import java.io.ByteArrayOutputStream;
import java.io.IOException;
import java.io.InputStream;
import java.util.List;
import java.util.Vector;
public class AppContent {

    public AppContent()
    {

    }

    public List<String> getContent(String contentId)
    {
        InputStream is = this.getClass().getClassLoader().
getResourceAsStream(
        "samples/"+contentId+".html");
        String content=streamToString(is);
        List<String> contentList=new Vector<String>();
        //Javascript within script tag will be extracted and sent
separately to client
        for(String script=getScript(content);!script.equals("");script=g
etScript(content))
        {
            contentList.add(script);
            content=removeScript(content);
```

```
    }
    //content list will have all the javascript
    //functions, last element is executed last
    //and all other before html content
    if(contentList.size()>1)
    {
        contentList.add(contentList.size()-1, content);
    }
    else
    {
        contentList.add(content);
    }
    return contentList;
}

public List<String> getLetters()
{
    List<String> letters=new Vector<String>();
    char[] l=new char[1];
    for(int i=65;i<91;i++)
    {
        l[0]=(char)i;
        letters.add(new String(l));
    }
    return letters;
}

public String removeScript(String html)
{
    //removes first script element
    int sIndex=html.toLowerCase().indexOf("<script ");
    if(sIndex==-1)
    {
        return html;
    }
    int eIndex=html.toLowerCase().indexOf("</script>")+9;
    return html.substring(0, sIndex)+html.substring(eIndex);
}

public String getScript(String html)
{
    //returns first script element
    int sIndex=html.toLowerCase().indexOf("<script ");
    if(sIndex==-1)
    {
        return "";
    }
```

```
        int eIndex=html.toLowerCase().indexOf("</script>")+9;
        return html.substring(sIndex, eIndex);
    }

    public String streamToString(InputStream is)
    {
        String content="";
        try
        {
        ByteArrayOutputStream baos=new ByteArrayOutputStream();
        for(int b=is.read();b!=-1;b=is.read())
        {
            baos.write(b);
        }
        content=baos.toString();
        }
        catch(IOException ioe)
        {
            content=ioe.toString();
        }
        return content;
    }
}
```

The `getContent()` method reads the HTML code from a file based on the `contentId`. `ContentId` was specified in the `dwrapplication.properties` file, and the HTML is just `contentId` plus the extension `.html` in the package directory. There is also a `getLetters()` method that simply lists letters from A to Z and returns a list of letters to the browser.

If we test the application now, we will get an error as shown in the following screenshot:

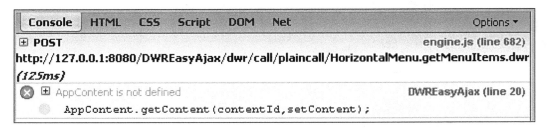

We know why the **AppContent is not defined** error occurs, so lets fix it by adding AppContent to the allow element in the dwr.xml file. We also add CountryDB to the allow element. The first thing we do is to add required elements to the dwr.xml file. We add the following creators within the allow element in the dwr.xml file.

```
<create creator="new" javascript="AppContent">
  <param name="class" value="samples.AppContent" />
  <include method="getContent" />
  <include method="getLetters" />
</create>
<create creator="new" javascript="CountryDB">
  <param name="class" value="samples.CountryDB" />
  <include method="getCountries" />
  <include method="saveCountryNotes" />
  <include method="getCountryData" />
</create>
```

We explicitly define the methods we are remoting using the include elements. This is a good practice, as we don't accidentally allow access to any methods that are not meant to be remoted.

Client Code for Tables and Lists

We also need to add a JavaScript interface to the index.jsp page. Add the following with the rest of the scripts in the index.jsp file.

```
<script type='text/javascript' src='/DWREasyAjax/dwr/interface/
AppContent.js'></script>
```

Before testing, we need the sample HTML for the content area. The following HTML is in the TablesAndLists.html file under the **samples** directory:

```
<h3>Countries</h3>
<p>Show countries starting with
<select id="letters" onchange="selectLetter(this);return false;"> </
select><br/>
Doubleclick "Notes"-cell to add notes to country.
</p>
<table border="1">
  <thead>
    <tr>
      <th>Name</th>
      <th>Long name</th>
      <th>Code</th>
    <th>Capital</th>
      <th>Notes</th>
    </tr>
```

```
    </thead>
    <tbody id="countryData">
    </tbody>
</table>

<script type='text/javascript'>
//TO BE EVALED
AppContent.getLetters(addLetters);
</script>
```

The `script` element at the end is extracted by our Java class, and it is then evaluated by the browser when the client-side JavaScript receives the HTML. There is the `select` element, and its `onchange` event calls the `selectLetter()` JavaScript function. We will implement the `selectLetter()` function shortly.

JavaScript functions are added in the `index.jsp` file, and within the `head` element. Functions could be in separate JavaScript files, but the embedded script is just fine here.

```
function selectLetter(selectElement)
{
  var selectedIndex = selectElement.selectedIndex;
  var selectedLetter= selectElement.options[selectedIndex ].value;
  CountryDB.getCountries(selectedLetter,setCountryRows);
}
function addLetters(letters)
{
dwr.util.addOptions('letters',['letter...']);
dwr.util.addOptions('letters',letters);
}

function setCountryRows(countryData)
{
var cellFuncs = [
  function(data) { return data[0]; },
  function(data) { return data[1]; },
  function(data) { return data[2]; },
  function(data) { return data[3]; },
  function(data) { return data[4]; }
];
dwr.util.removeAllRows('countryData');
dwr.util.addRows( 'countryData',countryData,cellFuncs, {

  cellCreator:function(options) {
    var td = document.createElement("td");
    if(options.cellNum==4)
    {
      var notes=options.rowData[4];
      if(notes==undefined)
```

```
      {
        notes=' ';// + options.rowData[2]+'notes';
      }
      var ccode=options.rowData[2];
      var divId=ccode+'_Notes';
      var tdId=divId+'Cell';
      td.setAttribute('id',tdId);
      var html=getNotesHtml(ccode,notes);
      td.innerHTML=html;
      options.data=html;
    }
    return td;
  },
  escapeHtml:false
 });
}

function getNotesHtml(ccode,notes)
{
  var divId=ccode+'_Notes';
  return "<div onDblClick=
          \"editCountryNotes('"+divId+"','"+ccode+"');\" id=
                              \""+divId+"\">"+notes+"</div>";
}

function editCountryNotes(id,ccode)
{
  var notesElement=dwr.util.byId(id);
  var tdId=id+'Cell';
  var notes=notesElement.innerHTML;
  if(notes==' ')
  {
    notes='';
  }
  var editBox='<input id="'+ccode+'NotesEditBox" type=
                          "text" value="'+notes+'"/><br/>';
  editBox+="<input type='button' id='"+ccode+"SaveNotesButton'
          value='Save' onclick='saveCountryNotes(\""+ccode+"\");'/>";
  editBox+="<input type='button' id='"+ccode+"CancelNotesButton'
              value='Cancel' onclick='cancelEditNotes
                                      (\""+ccode+"\");'/>";
  tdElement=dwr.util.byId(tdId);
  tdElement.innerHTML=editBox;
  dwr.util.byId(ccode+'NotesEditBox').focus();
}
```

```
function cancelEditNotes(ccode)
{
  var countryData=CountryDB.getCountryData(ccode, {
  callback:function(data)
  {
    var notes=data[4];
    if(notes==undefined)
    {
      notes=' ';
    }
    var html=getNotesHtml(ccode,notes);
    var tdId=ccode+'_NotesCell';
    var td=dwr.util.byId(tdId);
    td.innerHTML=html;
  }
  });

}
function saveCountryNotes(ccode)
{
  var editBox=dwr.util.byId(ccode+'NotesEditBox');
  var newNotes=editBox.value;
  CountryDB.saveCountryNotes(ccode,newNotes, {
  callback:function(newNotes)
  {
    var ccode=newNotes[0];
    var notes=newNotes[1];
    var notesHtml=getNotesHtml(ccode,notes);
    var td=dwr.util.byId(ccode+"_NotesCell");
    td.innerHTML=notesHtml;
  }
  });
}
```

There are lots of functions for table samples, and we go through each one of them.

The first is the `selectLetter()` function. This function gets the selected letter from the `select` element and calls the `CountryDB.getCountries()` remoted Java method. The callback function is `setCountryRows`. This function receives the return value from the Java `getCountries()` method, that is `List<List<String>>`, a `List` of `Lists` of `Strings`.

The second function is `addLetters(letters)`, and it is a callback function for the `AppContent.getLetters()` method, which simply returns letters from A to Z. The `addLetters()` function uses the DWR utility functions to populate the letter list.

Then there is a callback function for the `CountryDB.getCountries()` method. The parameter for the function is an array of countries that begin with a specified letter. Each array element has a format: **Name**, **Long name**, (country code) **Code**, **Capital**, **Notes**. The purpose of this function is to populate the table with country data; and let's see how it is done. The variable, `cellFuncs`, holds functions for retrieving data for each cell in a column. The parameter named data is an array of country data that was returned from the Java class.

The table is populated using the DWR utility function, `addRows()`. The `cellFuncs` variable is used to get the correct data for the table cell. The `cellCreator` function is used to create custom HTML for the table cell. Default implementation generates just a `td` element, but our custom implementation generates the `td`-element with the `div` placeholder for user notes.

The `getNotesHtml()` function is used to generate the `div` element with the event listener for double-click.

The `editCountryNotes()` function is called when the table cell is double-clicked. The function creates input fields for editing notes with the **Save** and **Cancel** buttons.

The `cancelEditNotes()` and `saveCountryNotes()` functions cancel the editing of new notes, or saves them by calling the `CountryDB.saveCountryNotes()` Java method.

The following screenshot shows what the sample looks like with the populated table:

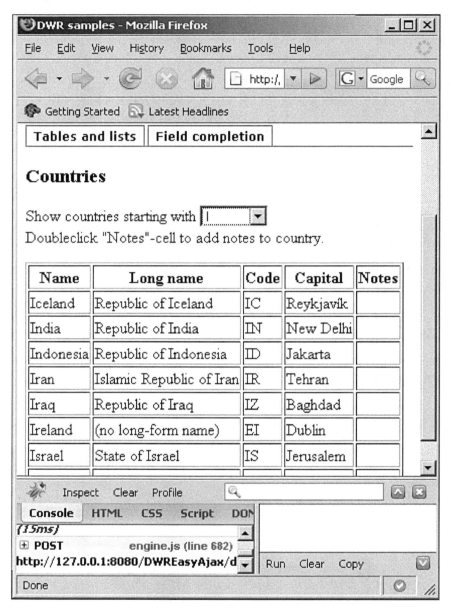

Now that we have added necessary functions to the web page we can test the application.

Testing Tables and Lists

The application should be ready for testing if we have had the test environment running during development. Eclipse automatically deploys our new code to the server whenever something changes. So we can go right away to the test page `http://127.0.0.1:8080/DWREasyAjax`. On clicking **Tables and lists** we can see the page we have developed. By selecting some letter, for example "I" we get a list of all the countries that start with letter "I" (as shown in the previous screenshot).

Now we can add notes to countries. We can double-click any table cell under **Notes**. For example, if we want to enter notes to **Iceland**, we double-click the **Notes** cell in Iceland's table row, and we get the edit box for the notes as shown in the following screenshot:

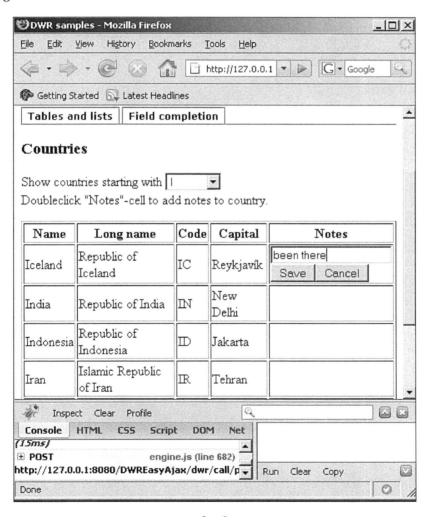

The edit box is a simple text input field. We didn't use any forms. Saving and canceling editing is done using JavaScript and DWR. If we press **Cancel**, we get the original notes from the `CountryDB` Java class using DWR and saving also uses DWR to save data. `CountryDB.saveCountryNotes()` takes the country code and the notes that the user entered in the edit box and saves them to the CSV file. When notes are available, the application will show them in the country table together with other country information as shown in the following screenshot:

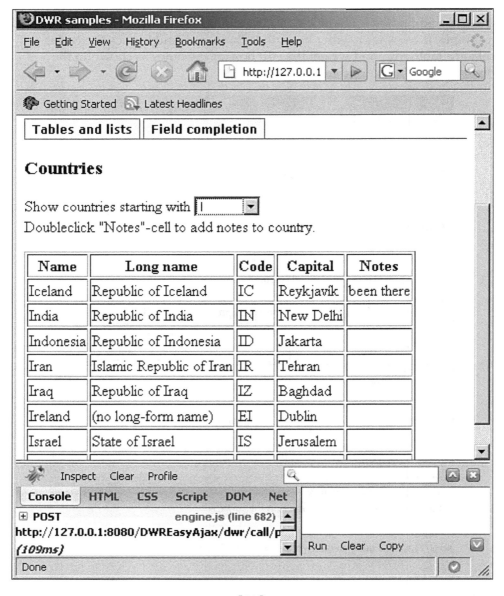

Afterword

The sample in this section uses DWR features to get data for the table and list from the server. We developed the application so that most of the application logic is written in JavaScript and Java beans that are remoted. In principle, the application logic can be thought of as being fully browser based, with some extensions in the server.

Implementing Field Completion

Nowadays, field completion is typical of many web pages. A typical use case is getting a stock quote, and field completion shows matching symbols as users type letters. Many Internet sites use this feature.

Our sample here is a simple license text finder. We enter the license name in the input text field, and we use DWR to show the license names that start with the typed text. A list of possible completions is shown below the input field. The following is a screenshot of the field completion in action:

Selected license content is shown in an `iframe` element from
`http://www.opensource.org`.

Server Code for Field Completion

We will re-use some of the classes we developed in the last section. `AppContent` is
used to load the sample page, and the `DBUtils` class is used in the `LicenseDB` class.
The `LicenseDB` class is shown here:

```java
package samples;

import java.util.List;
import java.util.Vector;

public class LicenseDB{

    private DBUtils dbUtils=new DBUtils();

    public LicenseDB()
    {
        dbUtils.initFileDB("licenses.csv");
    }

    public List<String> getLicensesStartingWith(String startLetters)
    {
        List<String> list=new Vector<String>();
        List<String> licenses=dbUtils.getCSVStrings(startLetters);
        for(String license : licenses)
        {
            list.add(license.split(",")[0]);
        }
        return list;
    }

    public String getLicenseContentUrl(String licenseName)
    {
        List<String> licenses=dbUtils.getCSVStrings(licenseName);
        if(licenses.size()>0)
        {
            return licenses.get(0).split(",")[1];
        }
        return "";
    }
}
```

The `getLicenseStartingWith()` method goes through the license names and returns valid license names and their URLs. Similar to the data in the previous section, license data is in a CSV file named `licenses.csv` in the package directory. The following is an excerpt of the file content:

```
Academic Free License, http://opensource.org/licenses/afl-3.0.php
Adaptive Public License, http://opensource.org/licenses/apl1.0.php
Apache Software License, http://opensource.org/licenses/apachep1-1.1.php
Apache License, http://opensource.org/licenses/apache2.0.php
Apple Public Source License, http://opensource.org/licenses/apsl-2.0.php
Artistic license, http://opensource.org/licenses/artistic-
license-1.0.php
...
```

There are quite a few open-source licenses. Some are more popular than others (like the Apache Software License) and some cannot be re-used (like the IBM Public License).

We want to remote the `LicenseDB` class, so we add the following to the `dwr.xml` file.

```
<create creator="new" javascript="LicenseDB">
  <param name="class" value="samples.LicenseDB"/>
  <include method="getLicensesStartingWith"/>
  <include method="getLicenseContentUrl"/>
</create>
```

Client Code for Field Completion

The following `script` element will go in the `index.jsp` page.

```
<script type='text/javascript' src='/DWREasyAjax/dwr/interface/
LicenseDB.js'></script>
```

The HTML for the field completion is as follows:

```
<h3>Field completion</h3>
<p>Enter Open Source license name to see it's contents.
</p>
<input type="text" id="licenseNameEditBox" value="" onkeyup="showPopup
Menu()"  size="40"/>
<input type="button" id="showLicenseTextButton" value="Show license
text"  onclick="showLicenseText()"/>
<div id="completionMenuPopup"></div>
<div id="licenseContent"></div>
```

The `input` element, where we enter the license name, listens to the `onkeyup` event which calls the `showPopupMenu()` JavaScript function. Clicking the Input button calls the `showLicenseText()` function (the JavaScript functions are explained shortly). Finally, the two `div` elements are place holders for the pop-up menu and the `iframe` element that shows license content.

For the pop-up box functionality, we use existing code and modify it for our purpose (many thanks to `http://www.jtricks.com`). The following is the `popup.js` file, which is located under the **WebContent | js** directory.

```
//<script type="text/javascript"><!--
/* Original script by: www.jtricks.com
 * Version: 20070301
 * Latest version:
 * www.jtricks.com/javascript/window/box.html
 *
 * Modified by Sami Salkosuo.
 */
// Moves the box object to be directly beneath an object.
function move_box(an, box)
{
    var cleft = 0;
    var ctop = 0;
    var obj = an;

    while (obj.offsetParent)
    {
        cleft += obj.offsetLeft;
        ctop += obj.offsetTop;
        obj = obj.offsetParent;
    }

    box.style.left = cleft + 'px';

    ctop += an.offsetHeight + 8;

    // Handle Internet Explorer body margins,
    // which affect normal document, but not
    // absolute-positioned stuff.
    if (document.body.currentStyle &&
        document.body.currentStyle['marginTop'])
    {
        ctop += parseInt(
            document.body.currentStyle['marginTop']);
    }
```

```
        box.style.top = ctop + 'px';
}

var popupMenuInitialised=false;
// Shows a box if it wasn't shown yet or is hidden
// or hides it if it is currently shown
function show_box(html, width, height, borderStyle,id)
{
    // Create box object through DOM
    var boxdiv = document.getElementById(id);
    boxdiv.style.display='block';
    if(popupMenuInitialised==false)
    {
      //boxdiv = document.createElement('div');
      boxdiv.setAttribute('id', id);
      boxdiv.style.display = 'block';
      boxdiv.style.position = 'absolute';
      boxdiv.style.width = width + 'px';
      boxdiv.style.height = height + 'px';
      boxdiv.style.border = borderStyle;
      boxdiv.style.textAlign = 'right';
      boxdiv.style.padding = '4px';
      boxdiv.style.background = '#FFFFFF';
      boxdiv.style.zIndex='99';
      popupMenuInitialised=true;
      //document.body.appendChild(boxdiv);
    }

    var contentId=id+'Content';
    var contents = document.getElementById(contentId);
    if(contents==null)
    {
      contents = document.createElement('div');
      contents.setAttribute('id', id+'Content');
      contents.style.textAlign= 'left';
      boxdiv.contents = contents;
      boxdiv.appendChild(contents);

    }
    move_box(html, boxdiv);

    contents.innerHTML= html;

    return false;
}
```

```
function hide_box(id)
{
    document.getElementById(id).style.display='none';
    var boxdiv = document.getElementById(id+'Content');
    if(boxdiv!=null)
    {
      boxdiv.parentNode.removeChild(boxdiv);

    }
    return false;
}

//--></script>
```

Functions in the `popup.js` file are used as menu options directly below the edit box.

The `show_box()` function takes the following arguments: HTML code for the pop-up, position of the pop-up window, and the "parent" element (to which the pop-up box is related). The function then creates a pop-up window using DOM. The `move_box()` function is used to move the pop-up window to its correct place under the edit box and the `hide_box()` function hides the pop-up window by removing the pop-up window from the DOM tree.

In order to use functions in `popup.js`, we need to add the following `script`-element to the `index.jsp` file:

```
<script type='text/javascript' src='js/popup.js'></script>
```

Our own JavaScript code for the field completion is in the `index.jsp` file. The following are the JavaScript functions, and an explanation follows the code:

```
function showPopupMenu()
{
  var licenseNameEditBox=dwr.util.byId('licenseNameEditBox');
  var startLetters=licenseNameEditBox.value;
  LicenseDB.getLicensesStartingWith(startLetters, {
  callback:function(licenses)
  {
    var html="";
    if(licenses.length==0)
    {
      return;
    }
    if(licenses.length==1)
    {
      hidePopupMenu();
```

```
            licenseNameEditBox.value=licenses[0];
          }
          else
          {
            for (index in licenses)
            {
              var licenseName=licenses[index];//.split(",")[0];
              licenseName=licenseName.replace(/\"/g,"&quot;");
              html+="<div style=\"border:1px solid #777777;
                        margin-bottom:5;\" onclick=
                                    \"completeEditBox('"+licenseName+"');
                                           \">"+licenseName+"</div>";
            }
            show_box(html, 200, 270, '1px solid','completionMenuPopup');
          }
        }
      });
    }

function hidePopupMenu()
{
  hide_box('completionMenuPopup');
}

function completeEditBox(licenseName)
{
  var licenseNameEditBox=dwr.util.byId('licenseNameEditBox');
  licenseNameEditBox.value=licenseName;
  hidePopupMenu();
  dwr.util.byId('showLicenseTextButton').focus();
}

function showLicenseText()
{
  var licenseNameEditBox=dwr.util.byId('licenseNameEditBox');
  licenseName=licenseNameEditBox.value;
  LicenseDB.getLicenseContentUrl(licenseName,{
  callback:function(licenseUrl)
  {
    var html='<iframe src="'+licenseUrl+'" width="100%"
                                        height="600"></iframe>';
    var content=dwr.util.byId('licenseContent');
    content.style.zIndex="1";
    content.innerHTML=html;
  }
  });
}
```

The `showPopupMenu()` function is called each time a user enters a letter in the input box. The function gets the value of the input field and calls the `LicenseDB`. `getLicensesStartingWith()` method. The callback function is specified in the function parameters. The callback function gets all the licenses that match the parameter, and based on the length of the parameter (which is an array), it either shows a pop-up box with all the matching license names, or, if the array length is one, hides the pop-up box and inserts the full license name in the text field. In the pop up box, the license names are wrapped within the `div` element that has an `onclick` event listener that calls the `completeEditBox()` function.

The `hidePopupMenu()` function just closes the pop-up menu and the `competeEditBox()` function inserts the clicked license text in the input box and moves the focus to the button. The `showLicenseText()` function is called when we click the **Show license text** button. The function calls the `LicenseDB`. `getLicenseContentUrl()` method and the callback function creates an `iframe` element to show the license content directly from `http://www.opensource.org`, as shown in the following screenshot:

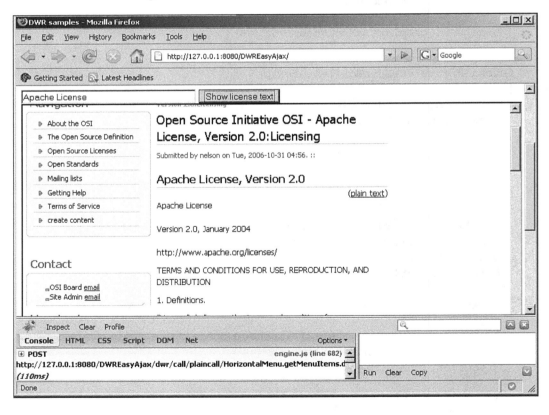

Afterword

Field completion improves user experience in web pages and the sample code in this section showed one way of doing it using DWR.

It should be noted that the sample for field completion presented here is only for demonstration purposes.

Summary

This chapter provided samples for a couple of common tasks that are used in web development: tables and lists, field completion, and even a generic frame, called a dynamic user interface, for our sample code. Both the tables and lists sample and the field completion sample had a very simple CSV-based "database" that holds the data for our purposes, and both had a remoted method that DWR uses to get the data from the server and show it in the client.

We also saw some good examples of HTML, CSS, and JavaScript. In fact, without knowledge of JavaScript it would be difficult to write web applications.

Many years ago, as some of you may remember, JavaScript was a dirty word in web development and no self-respecting developer would touch JavaScript. But change is a part of life, and in this case, change has been for the better. JavaScript and Java work very well together with the DWR in between.

The next chapter continues with the user interface part, and shows a couple more samples, including a map scrolling functionality, similar to what is found in the popular Google Maps website.

5
User Interface: Advanced Elements

This chapter has three samples: forms, navigation tree, and map scrolling. Forms are found in almost all the web applications, and the sample shows how to do form validation and processing using DWR. The navigation tree includes a simple navigation tree that has a Java bean for holding menu elements that are accessed via DWR. The last sample in this chapter is a map scrolling sample that shows how to achieve zooming and scrolling of a map using Java, JavaScript, and DWR.

The following are the sections discussed in this chapter:

- Creating Forms—includes examples of form processing
- Building a Navigation Tree—shows one way of using DWR in the navigation tree implementation
- Map Scrolling Using DWR—shows the DWR functionality in a web page map (from the planet Mars in this sample)

Creating Forms

This sample is about forms, form validation, and submission of a form. For this sample, the form we will handle is very simple, just a few fields, and the point of this sample is to show form validation using DWR and form submission using DWR. The form will appear as shown in the following screenshot:

DWR Easy Java Ajax Applications

| Tables and lists | Field completion | Form handling |

Form handling

Simple order form.

Name	
Address	
Credit card # use test number	
Credit card expiry (mm/yy)	
	Submit order

The **Name** and **Address** fields are nothing special, except maybe that the address field in real-life is virtually never a simple text field. The **Credit card** number is validated when it is entered in the input field. The **Credit card expiry** field is also validated when it is entered.

Developing the User Interface

The first thing to do is to add new menu items to the Dynamic User Interface that we had designed in the previous chapter. This is done by adding properties for menu items to the dwrapplication.properties file. We have already added menu items for the navigation tree and the map scrolling samples that we will develop later in this chapter:

```
menu.3=Form handling,FormHandling
menu.4=Navigation tree,NavigationTree
menu.5=Map scrolling,MapScrolling
```

The HTML code for our FormHandling.html file looks like this:

```
<h3>Form handling</h3>
<p>Simple order form.</p>
<div id="formFeedback"></div>
<table border="1" cellspacing="5" cellpadding="5">
  <tr>
    <td>Name</td>
    <td><input type="text" id="nameEditBox" value=""
  size="40" /></td>
```

```
    </tr>
    <tr>
      <td>Address</td>
      <td><input type="text" id="addressEditBox" value=""
    size="40" /></td>
    </tr>
    <tr>
      <td>Credit card #<br/><a href="#" onclick="useTestCreditCardNumber
();return false;">use test number</a></td>
      <td><input type="text" id="creditCardEditBox" value=""
    onkeyup="isValidCreditCard()" size="40" /></td>
    </tr>
    <tr>
      <td>Credit card expiry (mm/yy)</td>
      <td><input type="text" id="expiryEditBox" value=""
    onkeyup="checkExpiryDate()" size="40" /></td>
    </tr>
      <tr>
      <td> </td>
      <td><input type="button" id="submitOrderButton"
    value="Submit order" onclick="submitOrder()" /></td>
    </tr>
</table>
```

JavaScript functions are specified in the credit card number and expiry date input field `onkeyup` events and the `onclick` events of the use test number link and the submit-button. The following JavaScript functions are in the `index.jsp` file:

```
function useTestCreditCardNumber()
{
  var creditCardEditBox=dwr.util.byId('creditCardEditBox');
  creditCardEditBox.value='5555555555554444';
}

function isValidCreditCard()
{
  var creditCardEditBox=dwr.util.byId('creditCardEditBox');
  creditCardNumber=creditCardEditBox.value;
  FormHandler.isValidCreditCard(creditCardNumber,{
  callback:function(valid)
  {
    var feedback=dwr.util.byId('formFeedback');
    var html="";
    if(!valid)
    {
      html='<p><font color="red">Credit card number is not valid.</
font></p>';
    }
    feedback.innerHTML=html;
  }
```

```
    });
  }

  function checkExpiryDate()
  {
    var expiryEditBox=dwr.util.byId('expiryEditBox');
    expiryDate=expiryEditBox.value;
    FormHandler.checkExpiryFormat(expiryDate,{
    callback:function(valid)
    {
      var feedback=dwr.util.byId('formFeedback');
      var html="";
      if(!valid)
      {
        html='<p><font color="red">Expiry date is not in correct
                                          format.</font></p>';
      }
      feedback.innerHTML=html;
    }
    });
  }

  function submitOrder()
  {
    var creditCardEditBox=dwr.util.byId('creditCardEditBox');
    creditCardNumber=creditCardEditBox.value;
    var expiryEditBox=dwr.util.byId('expiryEditBox');
    expiryDate=expiryEditBox.value;
    var nameEditBox=dwr.util.byId('nameEditBox');
    name=nameEditBox.value;
    var addressEditBox=dwr.util.byId('addressEditBox');
    address=addressEditBox.value;

    FormHandler.submitOrder(name,address,creditCardNumber,expiryDate,{
    callback:function(orderSubmitted)
    {
      var feedback=dwr.util.byId('formFeedback');
      var html="";
      if(orderSubmitted)
      {
        html='<p><font color="green">Order submitted.</font></p>';
      }
      else
      {
        html='<p><font color="red">Order submit failed.</font></p>';

      }
      feedback.innerHTML=html;
    }
    });
  }
```

The first function, useTestCreditCardNumber, inserts a test number into the credit card field, so we don't have to use our own card number.

The isValidCreditCard() function is called when something is entered in the credit card input field. The function calls a server-side Java method (to be implemented shortly) and receives either true or false. If the credit card number fails the validation, the user is informed by changing the content of the div element with the formFeedback ID.

The checkExpiryDate() function is similar to the previous function except that it checks the expiry date syntax.

The last function is the submitOrder() function that reads form field values and calls the submitOrder() method in a remoted Java class. The Java method returns true or false, and the status of order submission is shown to the user.

Creating the FormHandler Class

The next thing to do is the FormHandler Java class. The implementation of the class is as follows:

```java
package samples;

public class FormHandler {

    public boolean submitOrder(String name,String address,String
creditCardNumber,String expiryDate)
    {
        boolean validExpiryDate=checkExpiryFormat(expiryDate);
        boolean validCreditCardNumber=
                            isValidCreditCard(creditCardNumber);
        //submit order to orderprocessing system
        boolean orderSubmitted=true;

        return validCreditCardNumber && validExpiryDate &&
                                            orderSubmitted;
    }

    public boolean checkExpiryFormat(String expiryDate) {
        if (expiryDate.length() != 5) {
            return false;
        }
        if (expiryDate.indexOf("/") == -1) {
            return false;
        }
```

```java
        String[] expDate = expiryDate.split("/");
        try {
            int month = Integer.parseInt(expDate[0]);
            int year = Integer.parseInt(expDate[1]);
            if ((month >= 1 && month <= 12) && (year >= 8 && year
                <= 99)) {
                return true;
            }
            return false;
        } catch (Exception e) {
            e.printStackTrace();
            return false;
        }
    }
    /*
     * The next two methods perform credit card validation.
     * Only the format is checked, it is not checked
     * against a card holder.
     *
     * Methods provided by Michael Gilleland in his essay
     * "Anatomy of Credit Card Numbers"
     * http://www.merriampark.com/anatomycc.htm
     */
    private String getDigitsOnly(String s) {
        StringBuffer digitsOnly = new StringBuffer();
        char c;
        for (int i = 0; i < s.length(); i++) {
            c = s.charAt(i);
            if (Character.isDigit(c)) {
                digitsOnly.append(c);
            }
        }
        return digitsOnly.toString();
    }

    public boolean isValidCreditCard(String cardNumber) {
        String digitsOnly = getDigitsOnly(cardNumber);
        int sum = 0;
        int digit = 0;
        int addend = 0;
        boolean timesTwo = false;
```

```
for (int i = digitsOnly.length() - 1; i >= 0; i--) {
    digit = Integer.parseInt(digitsOnly.substring(i, i +
                             1));
    if (timesTwo) {
        addend = digit * 2;
        if (addend > 9) {
            addend -= 9;
        }
    } else {
        addend = digit;
    }
    sum += addend;
    timesTwo = !timesTwo;
}
int modulus = sum % 10;
return modulus == 0;
    }
}
```

The first method, submitOrder(), takes the name, address, and credit card info as parameters and validates the input before sending the order to the order-processing system (not implemented in this sample) and returns either true or false value based on whether the order was successful or not.

The second method, checkExpiryFormat(), takes the credit card expiry date as the parameter and validates that it is in the correct format, MM/YY where MM and YY are integers in the range of 1-12 and 8-99 (years 2008-2099) respectively.

The last two methods validate that the credit card number is in the correct format. The code is written by Michael Gilleland, and it was published in his essay *Anatomy of Credit Card Numbers* (http://www.merriampark.com/anatomycc.htm). The essay explains what all those numbers in a credit card are, and how to verify that a given number is really a credit card number using the Luhn algorithm (refer to the essay for more information).

Testing the Form

The next thing to do is to add FormHandler to the HTML page and the remoted class to dwr.xml. We add the following to the index.jsp file:

```
<script type='text/javascript' src=
            '/DWREasyAjax/dwr/interface/FormHandler.js'></script>
```

And we add the following to the `dwr.xml` file:

```
<create creator="new" javascript="FormHandler">
  <param name="class" value="samples.FormHandler"/>
  <include method="checkExpiryFormat"/>
  <include method="isValidCreditCard"/>
  <include method="submitOrder"/>
</create>
```

Now the order form is ready. It is a very simple order form, but the idea is clear. Form fields can be validated while the user is inputting the text. So when the user submits the form, it is most likely that all the fields are correct. The following screenshot shows the form filling procedure in progress:

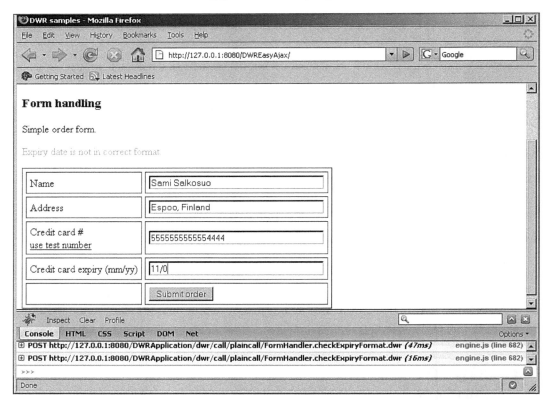

Note how the credit card expiry field is left incomplete. The Firebug window shows the DWR requests, and each time a character is entered in the field, the `checkExpiryFormat()` method is called. Note that, in this case, calling the server each time a character is entered introduces a lot of network traffic and overhead to the server code. However, in this sample, an illustrative example is worth the extra overhead on the server. Perhaps also in other cases, overhead may be considered secondary to good user experience and immediate feedback to the user.

When the fields are correct and the order is submitted, order is sent to the order processing system. After the order is completed, the user gets the confirmation for a successful order as shown in the following screenshot:

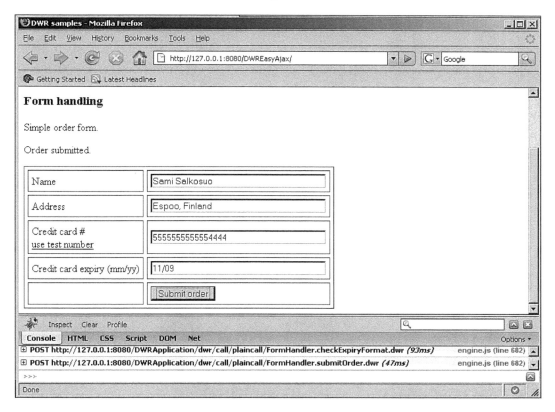

Of course, in real life, the user would get a receipt for the order instead of the green **Order submitted** text.

Afterword

The sample form in this section shows how DWR is used in form handling. DWR uses on forms include real-time validation of form fields. We also saw the algorithm to check the validity of the credit card number.

Building a Navigation Tree

This is a sample for building a navigation menu, where the menu contents are fetched from the server using DWR. The following is a screenshot of the menu we are developing in this section:

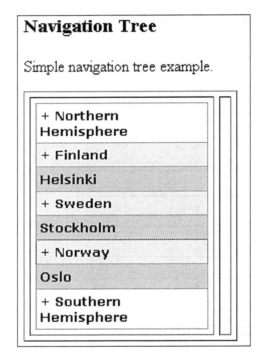

Developing the User Interface

We have already added the navigation tree menu item to dwrapplication. properties in the previous section, so we can start the development with the HTML file. The following HTML file is in the **samples** directory, and its name is NavigationTree.html.

```
<h3>Navigation Tree</h3>
<p>Simple navigation tree example.</p>
<table border="1" cellspacing="5" cellpadding="5">
```

```
  <tr>
    <td><div class="wireframemenu" id="treeMenu"></div></td>
    <td><div id="treeMenuContent"></div></td>
  </tr>
</table>

<script type='text/javascript'>
//TO BE EVALED
NavigationTree.getRootElements(createTreeMenu);
</script>
```

Note that the tree menu is in the `div` element with the `treeMenu` ID. It also has a style class, `wireframemenu`. This style is from the Dynamic Drive CSS library. The following styles are added to the `styles.css` file.

```
/*Credits: Dynamic Drive CSS Library */
/*URL: http://www.dynamicdrive.com/style/ */

.wireframemenu{
border: 1px solid #C0C0C0;
background-color: white;
border-bottom-width: 0;
width: 170px;
}

* html .wireframemenu{ /*IE only rule. Original menu width minus all
left/right paddings */
width: 164px;
}

.wireframemenu ul{
padding: 0;
margin: 0;
list-style-type: none;
}

.wireframemenu a{
font: bold 13px Verdana;
padding: 4px 3px;
display: block;
width: 100%; /*Define width for IE6's sake*/
color: #595959;
text-decoration: none;
border-bottom: 1px solid #C0C0C0;
}
```

```css
.wireframemenu a:visited{
color: #595959;
}

html>body .wireframemenu a{ /*Non IE rule*/
width: auto;
}

.wireframemenu a:hover{
background-color: #F8FBBD;
color: black;
}
```

Creating the NavigationTree Class

In the `NavigationTree.html` file, there was a JavaScript call to `NavigationTree.getRootElements()`. This is a remoted Java class, so let's implement the Java class. The source code is as shown:

```java
package samples;

import java.util.Hashtable;
import java.util.List;
import java.util.Map;
import java.util.Random;
import java.util.Vector;

public class NavigationTree {
    private String[] rootLevel={"Northern Hemisphere","Southern
Hemisphere"};

    private Map<String,List<String>> level_1=new Hashtable<String,List
<String>>();
    private Map<String,List<String>> level_2=new Hashtable<String,List
<String>>();

    private String[] ncap={"Helsinki","Stockholm","Oslo"};
    private String[] scap={"Wellington","Canberra","Port Louis"};

    public NavigationTree()
    {
        List<String> countries=new Vector<String>();
        //set northern hemisphere
        countries.add("Finland");
        countries.add("Sweden");
        countries.add("Norway");
```

```
        level_1.put(rootLevel[0], countries);
        for(int i=0;i<countries.size();i++)
        {
           Vector<String> capitals=new Vector<String>();
           capitals.add(ncap[i]);
           level_2.put(countries.get(i), capitals);
        }

        countries=new Vector<String>();
        countries.add("New Zealand");
        countries.add("Australia");
        countries.add("Mauritius");
        level_1.put(rootLevel[1], countries);
        for(int i=0;i<countries.size();i++)
        {
           Vector<String> capitals=new Vector<String>();
           capitals.add(scap[i]);
           level_2.put(countries.get(i), capitals);
        }
     }

     public String[] getRootElements()
     {
        return rootLevel;
     }

     public boolean hasChildren(String element)
     {
        return (level_1.containsKey(element) || level_2.containsKey
                                                      (element));
     }

     public List<String> getChildren(String element)
     {
        List<String> children=new Vector<String>();
        if(level_1.containsKey(element))
        {
           return level_1.get(element);
        }
        if(level_2.containsKey(element))
        {
           return level_2.get(element);
        }
```

```
        return children;
    }


    public String getContent(String element)
    {
        String[] desc={"A great place to be.","Nice place to
                        visit.","Good nightlife.","Excellent
                                    restaurants.","Unforgettable"};
        Random rnd=new Random();
        return "The capital is "+element+". "
                            +desc[rnd.nextInt(desc.length)];

    }
}
```

Our navigation tree here is hard-coded. Class variables include the root elements and the constructor populates the first-and second-level menus.

The getRootElements() method returns root elements. The hashChildren() method checks whether or not the given menu element has child elements, and the getChildren() method returns the child elements of the given element.

The last method, getContent(), just returns random content to the user interface.

Developing the User Interface, Part 2

Since we want to remote this Java class, we must update dwr.xml and index.jsp. Add the following to dwr.xml.

```
<create creator="new" javascript="NavigationTree">
  <param name="class" value="samples.NavigationTree" />
</create>
```

And then we add the following to index.jsp.

```
<script type='text/javascript' src='/DWREasyAjax/dwr/interface/
  NavigationTree.js'></script>
```

Now there is only one thing left. We have our Java, HTML, and configuration and we still need JavaScript functions so that everything works. In the NavigationTree. html file, there was already one named function, createTreeMenu(), which is a callback for the Java method call. The following are the functions for the navigation tree:

```
function createTreeMenu(rootElements)
{
    var treeMenu=dwr.util.byId('treeMenu');
```

```
var html="<ul>";

for (index in rootElements)
{
  var element=rootElements[index];
  NavigationTree.hasChildren(element,{
    async:false,
    callback:function(hasChildren)
    {
      if(hasChildren)
      {
        html+='<li><a href="#" onclick="expandElement(this);
                           return false;"> + '+element+'</a></li>';
      }
      else
      {
        html+='<li><a href="#" onclick="expandElement(this);
                           return false;">'+element+'</a></li>';
      }
    }
    });
}

html+="</ul>";
treeMenu.innerHTML=html;

}

function expandElement(element)
{
  var value=element.text.replace(' + ','');
  var html="";
  NavigationTree.getChildren(value,{
  async:false,
  callback:function(childElements)
  {
    for (index in childElements)
    {
      var element=childElements[index];
      NavigationTree.hasChildren(element,{
      async:false,
      callback:function(hasChildren)
      {
        if(hasChildren)
```

```
        {
          html+='<li><a href="#" onclick="expandElement(this);return
false;"> + '+element+'</a></li>';
        }
        else
        {
          html+='<li style="background-color:#dddddd"><a href="#" oncl
ick="showContent(this);return false;">'+element+'</a></li>';
        }
      }
      });
    }
  }
  });
  var parentNode=element.parentNode;
  var childNodes=parentNode.childNodes;
  if(childNodes.length>1)
  {
    for(var i=1;i<childNodes.length;i++)
    {
      parentNode.removeChild(childNodes[i]);
    }
    var treeMenuContent=dwr.util.byId('treeMenuContent');
    treeMenuContent.innerHTML="";
  }
  else
  {
    var ul = document.createElement("ul");
    ul.innerHTML=html;
    ul.style.backgroundColor="#eeeeee";
    parentNode.appendChild(ul);
  }
}

function showContent(element)
{
  var value=element.text.replace(' ','');
  NavigationTree.getContent(value,{
  callback:function(content)
  {
    var treeMenuContent=dwr.util.byId('treeMenuContent');
    treeMenuContent.innerHTML=content;
  }
  });
}
```

The first function is the callback for the `getRootElements()` Java call. The functionality of the function is to get root elements and, for each element, it checks the existence of child elements and, based on that, it writes the HTML code for the menu element. Note that the menus are `li` elements, and our styles for `wireframemenu` specify how the `li` elements have to be handled within our menu. We see a menu instead of a bulleted list. Make note of one parameter in the `NavigationTree.hasChildren()` remote call: that is `async:false`. This is interesting because it forces the call to the server to be synchronous, just like normal method calls in any given programming language. Care must be taken while using synchronous calls in A(synchronous)JAX–it may slow down the application considerably.

The next function is `expandElement()`. This also checks the child elements and writes new links to the menu or to the content.

The third function is `showContent()`. This calls the remoted Java method and retrieves the content of the given element.

And so this sample menu tree is ready. Although the menu is hard-coded, it will give a good starting point for developing a dynamic tree menu backed by a database or some other mechanism.

Testing the Navigation Tree

When we start the **Navigation Tree** sample, we get a top-level tree as shown in the following screenshot:

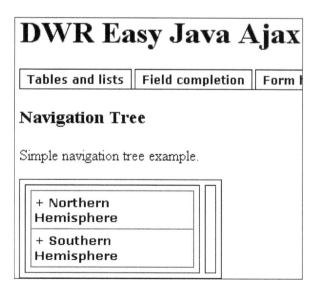

We can expand the menu elements as shown in the following two screenshots, where we first expand **Northern Hemisphere** and then we expand **Finland**. The capital of **Finland** is shown, and when we click it, we get its description.

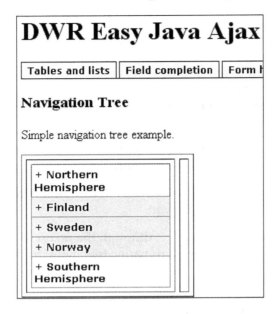

And when we expand **Finland** and click on **Helsinki**, we get the content as shown in the following screenshot:

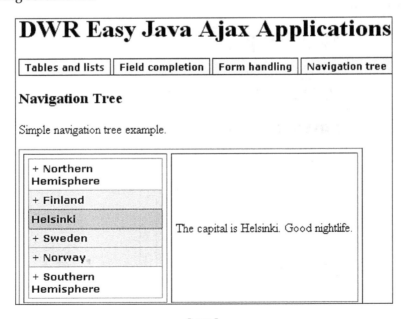

Afterword

This sample presented a navigation tree and how DWR is used to provide menu elements dynamically.

Map Scrolling Using DWR

The last sample in this chapter is a map scrolling sample using DWR. Browser-based, mouse-controlled scrolling maps have become popular since Google Maps was launched.

The principle idea, in the implementation of this sample, is to take a sufficiently large map and divide it to small squares of equal size. Then, based on the location, a certain number of the small squares are inserted into the visible map window, and when the user scrolls the map, by pressing the left mouse button, and dragging the mouse in the map window, new map squares are retrieved from the server (other implementations may also download map squares around the visible map window).

In this sample, we use a geological map of the Tempe-Mareotis region of Mars, provided by the U.S. Geological Survey Astrogeology Research Program (http://astrogeology.usgs.gov/). For a direct link to the map and additional information, refer to http://astrogeology.usgs.gov/Projects/MapBook/fulllisting.jsp?mapNumber=1170.

The following screenshot shows the full map of the Tempe-Mareotis region we are using in this sample.

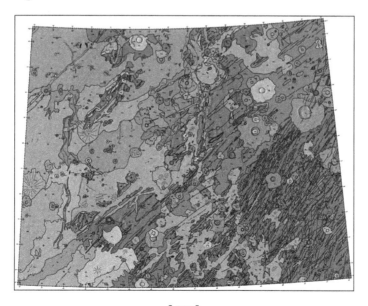

We use two zoom levels. The original image size for zoom level 0 is 1000x825 pixels and for zoom level 1 the image size is 2000x1632. Both original images are divided into squares of 100x100 pixels each, except the bottom part of the map since its height is not divisible by 100.

The following are a few random examples of map squares:

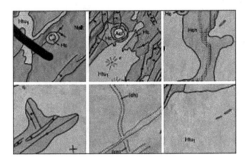

As the original pictures are quite large, there are a total of 90 map squares for zoom level 0 and 340 squares for zoom level 1.

The sample code shows how to use DWR and JavaScript to implement a scrolling map application. We develop an application as shown in the following screenshot. The image squares have borders in order to visualize how the map is constructed.

Developing the User Interface

We start development with the HTML file. The HTML code for the map scroller is as shown:

```
<h3>Map Scrolling</h3>
<p>Simple map scroller using geologic map of the Tempe-Mareotis Region
of Mars.<br/> Full description from <a href="http://astrogeology.usgs.
gov/Projects/MapBook/fulllisting.jsp?mapNumber=1170">here</a>.</p>
<div id="mapArea">
Zoom level: <form id="zoomLevelForm"><select id="zoomLevel" onchange="
setZoomLevel(this);return false;"><option>0</option><option>1</option>
</select></form><br/>
<iframe width="430" height="440" scrolling="no" frameborder="0"
src="MapArea.html">
</iframe>
</div>
```

The control element for zooming is a select box, and it uses the JavaScript function to set a new zoom level for the map. The setZoomLevel() function is in the index.jsp file. The function code is as follows:

```
function setZoomLevel(element)
{
  var selectedIndex = element.selectedIndex;
  var value= element.options[selectedIndex].value;
  var frames=window.frames;
  frames[0].setZoomLevel(value);
}
```

This function takes the select element, extracts a value from it, and calls the other setZoomLevel() function that is in the MapArea.html file.

The map area is an iframe element, and its source code is in a MapArea.html file, which is shown below. The source of the file is located in the **WebContent** directory.

```
<!DOCTYPE html PUBLIC "-//W3C//DTD HTML 4.01 Transitional//EN"
"http://www.w3.org/TR/html4/loose.dtd">
<html>
<head>
<script type='text/javascript'
  src='/DWREasyAjax/dwr/interface/MapScroller.js'></script>
<script type='text/javascript' src='/DWREasyAjax/dwr/engine.js'></
script>
<script type='text/javascript' src='/DWREasyAjax/dwr/util.js'></
script>
<script type="text/javascript">
```

```
var zoomLevel = 0;
var mapPositionIndex= 0;

var refGridX=0;
var refGridY=0;

function getRowIndex()
{
  var tempIndex=0;
    if(zoomLevel==0)
    {
      if(mapPositionIndex>=10)
      {
        tempIndex=parseInt(mapPositionIndex.toString().substring(1));
      }
      else
      {
        tempIndex=mapPositionIndex;
      }
    }
    else
    {
      if(mapPositionIndex>=100)
      {
        tempIndex=parseInt(mapPositionIndex.toString().substring(1));
      }
      else
      {
        tempIndex=mapPositionIndex;
      }
      while(tempIndex>16)
      {
        tempIndex-=20;
      }
      if(tempIndex<0)
      {
        tempIndex=16;
      }

    }
  return tempIndex;
}
```

```
function setZoomLevel(newZoomLevel)
{
  if(newZoomLevel==0)
  {
    oldMapPositionIndex=mapPositionIndex;
    newRow=Math.round(Math.round(mapPositionIndex/17.0)/2.0)-1;
    if(newRow>5)
    {
      newRow=5;
    }
    else
    {
      if(newRow>=1 && newRow<=5)
      {
        newRow--;
      }
    }
    newColumn=Math.floor(getRowIndex()/2.0)-1;
    if(newColumn>6)
    {
      newColumn=6;
    }
    mapPositionIndex=(newRow*10)+newColumn;
    if(oldMapPositionIndex==208)
    {
      mapPositionIndex=43;
    }
    if(oldMapPositionIndex==214)
    {
      mapPositionIndex=46;
    }
    if(mapPositionIndex<0)
    {
      mapPositionIndex=0;
    }
  }
  else
  {
    mapPositionIndex=(Math.floor(mapPositionIndex
                          /10.0)*40)+40+(2*(getRowIndex()+1));
  }
  zoomLevel=newZoomLevel;
  getMapImages(zoomLevel,mapPositionIndex);
}
```

```
function getMapImages(zoomLevel,mapPositionIndex)
{
  MapScroller.getMapImages(zoomLevel,mapPositionIndex, {
    callback:function(images) {
      setImages(images, zoomLevel);
    }
  });
}

function setRefGrid(event)
{
  refGridX=Math.floor(event.clientX/100.0);
  refGridY=Math.floor(event.clientY/100.0);
}

function startScroll(event)
{
  setRefGrid(event);
  document.addEventListener("mousemove", mouseMove,    true);
  document.addEventListener("mouseup",   stopScroll, true);
  document.addEventListener("mouseout",   stopScrollOnOut, true);
  document.addEventListener("mouseover",   stopScrollOnOut, true);
  event.preventDefault();
}

function stopScroll(event)
{
  document.removeEventListener("mousemove", mouseMove,    true);
  document.removeEventListener("mouseup",   stopScroll, true);
  document.removeEventListener("mouseout",   stopScrollOnOut, true);
  document.removeEventListener("mouseover",   stopScrollOnOut, true);
}

function stopScrollOnOut(event)
{
  var src=event.target;
  if(src.id=="scrollingMapArea")
  {
    stopScroll(event);
  }
}
```

```
function mouseMove(event)
{
  x=event.clientX;
  y=event.clientY;
  newGridX=Math.floor(x/100.0);
  newGridY=Math.floor(y/100.0);
  deltaX=newGridX-refGridX;
  deltaY=newGridY-refGridY;
  if(deltaX==0 && deltaY==0)
  {
    return;
  }
  var update=false;
  var tilesInRow=10;
  if(zoomLevel==1)
  {
    tilesInRow=20;
  }
  tempIndex=getRowIndex();

  if(deltaX>0)
  {
      if((tempIndex<6 && zoomLevel==0) || (tempIndex<16 &&
                                          zoomLevel==1))
      {
        mapPositionIndex++;
        update=true;
      }
  }
  else
  {
    if(deltaX<0)
    {
      if(tempIndex>0)
      {
        if(mapPositionIndex-1>=0)
        {
          mapPositionIndex--;
          update=true;
        }
      }

    }
  }
```

```
        if(deltaY>0)
        {
            var tempYIndex=50;
            if(zoomLevel==1)
            {
              tempYIndex=260;
            }
            if(mapPositionIndex<tempYIndex)
            {
              mapPositionIndex+=tilesInRow;
              update=true;
            }
        }
        else
        {
          if(deltaY<0)
          {
            if(mapPositionIndex>0 && mapPositionIndex>=tilesInRow)
            {
            mapPositionIndex-=tilesInRow;
            if(mapPositionIndex<0)
            {
               mapPositionIndex=0;
            }
            update=true;
          }
        }
      }

      if(update)
      {
        setRefGrid(event);
        getMapImages(zoomLevel,mapPositionIndex);
      }
    }

    function setImages(images,zoomLevel)
    {
      var mapArea=dwr.util.byId('scrollingMapArea');
      mapArea.innerHTML="";
      for(index in images)
      {
        var imageName=images[index];
        var mapPart = document.createElement("img");
        mapPart.setAttribute('border','1');
        mapPart.setAttribute('src','mapimages/'+imageName);
        mapArea.appendChild(mapPart);
      }
```

```
}
</script>
</head>
<body onMouseDown="startScroll(event)">
<div id="scrollingMapArea"></div>
</body>

<script type="text/javascript">
getMapImages(zoomLevel,mapPositionIndex);
</script>
</html>.
```

This HTML file holds everything related to map scrolling. In the body element there is a single div element that holds map squares. We remember that the iframe width and height are 430x430, and as map squares are 100x100, the map view port will have a total of 16 map images.

In the JavaScript code, the mapPositionIndex variable is an array index of the upper left corner of the view port. For example, when a map shows the upper left corner mapPositionIndex as 0, and it is scrolled row by row to the bottom, the mapPositionIndex changes to 10 (for zoom level 0) or 20 (for zoom level 1).

First, the getRowIndex() JavaScript function calculates which row is at the top of a visible view port.

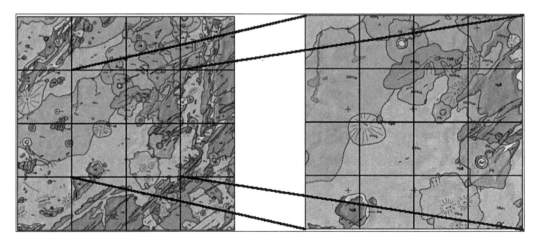

The second function, setZoomLevel(), is important. It calculates the mapPositionIndex for the new zoom level. When zooming in, four squares in the center will be zoomed visible, and when zooming out, the visible squares are in the center. The screenshot above is an example of how zooming is visible to the user. The left image is zoom level 0, and the image on the right is zoom level 1.

Using the `zoomLevel` and the `mapPositionIndex`, images are retrieved using the `getImages()` function. It just calls the remoted Java method, where the callback function for the Java method is `setImages()`.

The `setImages()` function receives an array of image names from the Java method, and it uses a `for` loop to create `img` elements, which are appended to the map area `div` element.

The `setRefGrid()`, `startScroll()`, `stopScroll()`, `stopScrollOnOut()`, and `mouseMove()` functions are used to handle map scrolling. The way scrolling works is that the `startScroll()` function is called when the user presses the mouse button down. The function then adds the event listeners for the `mousemove`, `mouseup`, `mouseout`, and `mouseover` events. While the mouse button is pressed down and the mouse is moved, then the `mouseMove()` function is called.

The `mouseMove()` function calculates the grid position the mouse is in (remember that the map view port was 4 by 4 squares). The reference position is set using the `setRefGrid()` function (this is also called when the button is pressed). If the mouse cursor has moved to a new grid position, then the `getImages()` function is called with the new `mapPositionIndex`, and the map squares are updated in the page.

When the mouse button is released, the `stopScroll()` function is called, and all event listeners are removed. This also happens when the user moves the mouse cursor outside the map area `div` element.

The actual map images are in the **WebContent | mapimages** directory. Map square images from zoom level 0 are `tempe-mareotis-zlevel-0-0.jpg` to `tempe-mareotis-zlevel-0-89.jpg`, and for zoom level 1, `tempe-mareotis-zlevel-1-0.jpg` to `tempe-mareotis-zlevel-1-339.jpg`, thereby taking it to well over 400 images for just two zoom levels.

Creating the MapScroller Java Class

Finally, we need the Java class that returns the image names. The Java code is as follows:

```java
package samples;

import java.util.List;
import java.util.Vector;

public class MapScroller {

    private int[] imagesInRowInZLevel = { 10, 20 };
    private String imageName = "tempe-mareotis-zlevel-";
```

```
public List<String> getMapImages(int zoomLevel,
                                 int mapPositionIndex) {
    List<String> images = new Vector<String>();
    String imageName = this.imageName + zoomLevel + "-";
    for (int rowIndex = 0; rowIndex < 4; rowIndex++) {
        for (int i = 0; i < 4; i++) {
            int index = mapPositionIndex + i;
            images.add(imageName + index + ".jpg");
        }
        mapPositionIndex = mapPositionIndex
                + imagesInRowInZLevel[zoomLevel];
    }
    return images;
}
}
```

There is only one method in the MapScroller class, getMapImages(). The method returns 16 image names for the current view in the HTML page. The parameter, mapPositionIndex, is the upper left corner of the image, and it is used to calculate the indexes of the other images.

Let's not forget to add the remoted class to the dwr.xml file:

```
<create creator="new" javascript="NavigationTree">
  <param name="class" value="samples.NavigationTree" />
</create>
```

This completes the map scrolling sample. Most of the functionality is in the browser-side JavaScript functions. But this kind of functionality would not be possible without AJAX. This appears to be a very simple implementation, and this is because DWR hides low-level details of asynchronous communication between the browser and the server, and allows us to develop the map scrolling functionality with just a few lines of server-side code in one Java class, and a bunch of map square images.

Testing the Map Scroller

The following three screenshots shows the map scroller in action. Note the mouse cursor and the hand-drawn arrow that shows the movement of the cursor.

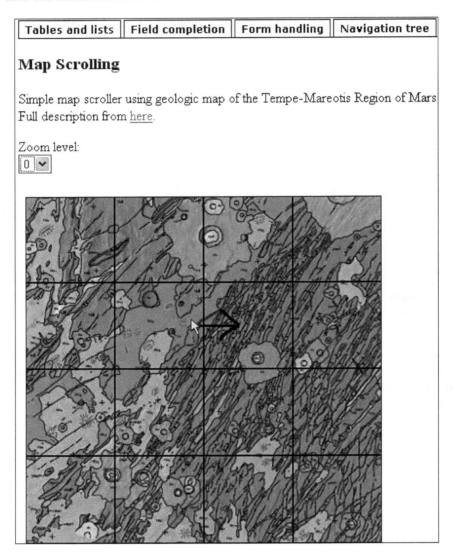

In this case, the mouse button is pressed down, and we move the cursor to the right. When the cursor crosses the black border, we know it because of the JavaScript code we have written, and it signals the map to scroll and update the images. After moving the mouse to the right in the screenshot and crossing the border, the map is scrolled to the right as is shown in the following screenshot:

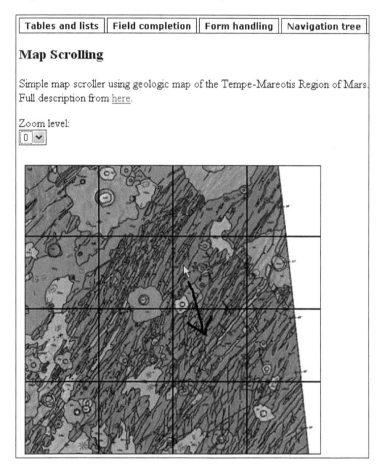

The previous screenshot also has a hand-drawn black arrow, and when we move the cursor down (with the button pressed down), when we cross the border again, the map scrolls down as shown in the following screenshot:

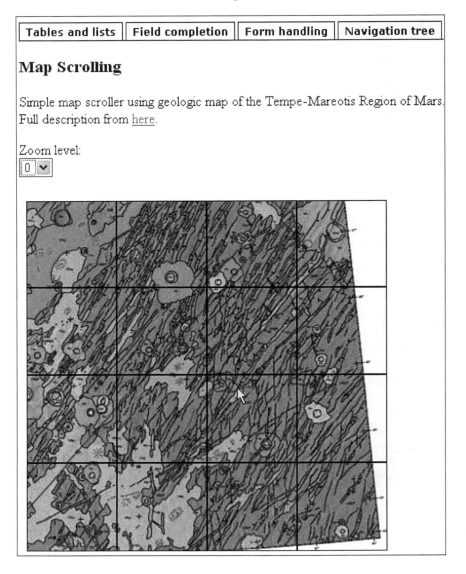

Afterword

This map scroller sample features a very user friendly method for scrolling maps or images. We also saw that the implementation is very client-centric because our server-side Java code (which was remoted) has only one class and one method.

Summary

This chapter presented user interface components that are available in many applications. Forms are present in all the applications that accept input from users. The navigation tree is user-friendly, and map scrolling is seen as a must in specific applications.

Using these user interface components is easy with DWR. DWR makes it possible to add very dynamic behavior to applications easily. Although the samples are more or less hard-coded, the principal ideas are presented, and sample code is a good starting point for not-so-hard-coded applications.

6
Backend Integration

This chapter is on integrating web applications with various backend services. Almost all applications involve a database, so the first example in this chapter shows one way of accessing database from the DWR application. The second example integrates with a standard web service while the third example uses JMS messaging to access a backend service. The JMS example also shows how to do Reverse AJAX (Comet) using DWR.

This chapter includes the following sections:

- Integrating a Database with DWR—shows how DWR is used to access a database
- Integrating with web services—uses Eclipse tooling to generate a web service client for our DWR application
- Integrating with a Messaging System—integrates our DWR application with the Python-based "order system" using Active MQ and JMS

Integrating a Database with DWR

Here, we integrate a database with DWR by exposing a database table via a remoted Java class. Our Java class connects directly to the database using JDBC, and related SQL statements are included in the class. Other ways to access databases include EJBs, Hibernate, and numerous others.

The example here replaces the first example in Chapter 4, Tables and Lists, so that country data comes from a database instead of a CSV file. From the application point of view there is only one change required in the dwr.xml file and that is changing the entry to point to the Java class that handles database access. Before we implement the Java class we have to set up and populate the database. Here we use Apache Derby database, which comes bundled with the Geronimo application server.

Configuring the Database in Geronimo

The first thing to do is to set up a database and table for our country data. This is easy when using Geronimo because it gives us the necessary tools for database management.

1. After logging into the **Geronimo console**, we go to **Embedded DB | DB Manager**.

2. In the **Run SQL** section (refer to the following screenshot) we create a new database by giving it a name and pressing the **Create** button. This creates a new database and then we can use the **SQL Command/s** text area to enter SQL commands that creates tables for our country data.

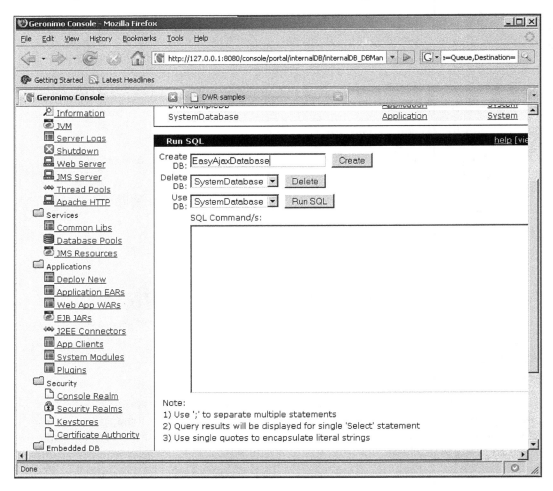

3. The following SQL command creates a country data table.

```
CREATE TABLE country_data (
        id INTEGER generated always as identity,
    short_name VARCHAR(64) NOT NULL,
    long_name VARCHAR(256) NOT NULL,
    code CHAR(2) NOT NULL,
    capital VARCHAR(64) NOT NULL,
    notes VARCHAR(256) DEFAULT ''
    );
ALTER TABLE country_data ADD CONSTRAINT pkey PRIMARY KEY (id);
```

4. Insert the SQL in the command area and hit the **Run SQL** button.

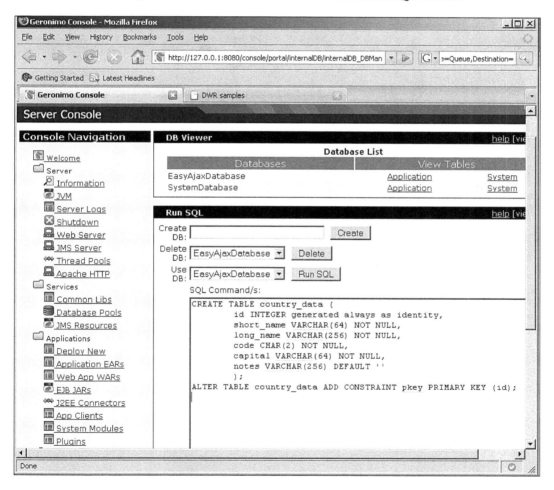

We can view tables in the database using the **Geronimo Console**. There
is a **Database List** shown in the following screenshot that has a link to view
application tables and contents of the tables:

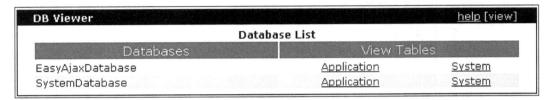

The application table that has a link to view the contents of the tables present
in the **Database List** is shown in the following screenshot:

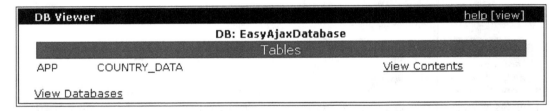

The contents of the table are as follows:

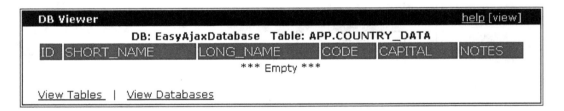

The table is empty and here is an excerpt of the SQL statements that
populate the table with country data:

```
insert into country_data (short_name,long_name,code,capital) values
('El Salvador','Republic of El Salvador','ES','San Salvador');
insert into country_data (short_name,long_name,code,capital) values
('Ethiopia','Federal DemocraticRepublic of Ethiopia','ET','Addis
Ababa');
insert into country_data (short_name,long_name,code,capital) values
('Fiji','Republic of theFiji Islands','FJ','Suva');
insert into country_data (short_name,long_name,code,capital) values
('Finland','Republic of Finland','FI','Helsinki');
...
```

After executing these commands in the DB manager, we see the contents of the table in the Geronimo **DB Viewer**.

DB Viewer					help [view]
DB: EasyAjaxDatabase Table: APP.COUNTRY_DATA					
ID	SHORT_NAME	LONG_NAME	CODE	CAPITAL	NOTES
1	Afghanistan	Islamic Republic of Afghanistan	AF	Kabul	
2	Albania	Republic of Albania	AL	Tirana	
3	Algeria	Peoples Democratic Republic of Algeria	AG	Algiers	
4	Andorra	Principality of Andorra	AN	Andorra la Vella	
5	Angola	Republic of Angola	AO	Luanda	
6	Antigua andBarbuda	(no long-form name)	AC	Saint Johns	
7	Argentina	Argentine Republic	AR	Buenos Aires	
8	Armenia	Republic of Armenia	AM	Yerevan	
9	Australia	Commonwealth of Australia	AS	Canberra	
10	Austria	Republic of Austria	AU	Vienna	
11	Azerbaijan	Republic of Azerbaijan	AJ	Baku	
12	Bahamas	The Commonwealth of The Bahamas	BF	Nassau	
13	Bahrain	Kingdom of Bahrain	BA	Manama	
14	Bangladesh	Peoples Republicof Bangladesh	BG	Dhaka	
15	Barbados	(no long-form name)	BB	Bridgetown	
16	Belarus	Republic of Belarus	BO	Minsk	

5. Now that we have the table and contents, we need the data source to access the content. We specify the data source in Geronimo and our Java class will use the server-provided data source to access the database. This way, Geronimo handles the nuts and bolts of the connectivity and also provides a pool of connections, which is good in case we have lots of concurrent users. The data source is specified in **Geronimo Console** in **Services | Database Pools**.

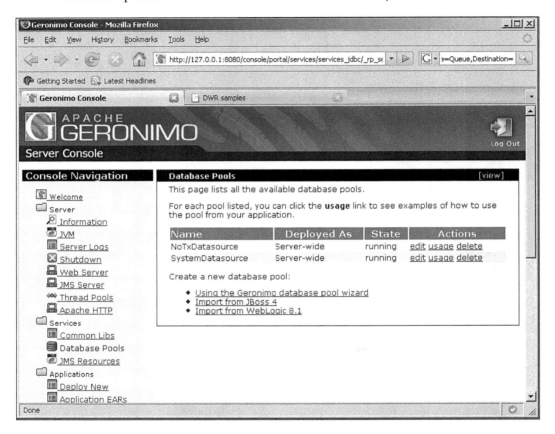

6. The new database pool is created using a wizard, which is found behind the **Using the Geronimo database pool wizard** link.

7. We use the name **EasyAjaxDBPool** as the database pool name, and the database type is **Derby network**.

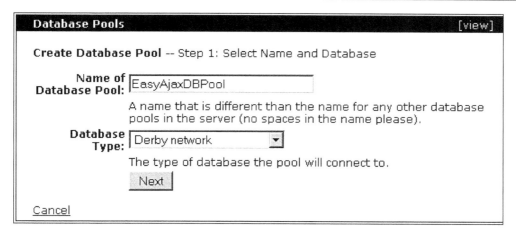

8. After clicking the **Next** button, there is a screen with a bunch of configuration entries.

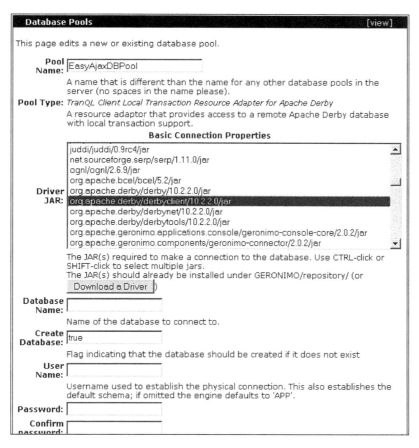

9. The JDBC driver that we use here is a client JAR for Derby, and is already available in the list of JDBC drivers. **Database Name** is what we defined earlier, **EasyAjaxDatabase**. We use **APP** as the username and **password** as the password. All other values can be default, so we can deploy the pool to Geronimo by pressing the **Deploy** button at the bottom of the screen.

Creating a CountryDerbyDB Java Class

Now, we have the data source for the database, and we can use it in our application. The next thing we do is create a new Java class for accessing the database, and after that we need to set up the application for accessing the data source in the Geronimo environment.

The Java class is CountryDerbyDB, and the source code for the class is as follows:

```
package samples;

import java.sql.Connection;
import java.sql.PreparedStatement;
import java.sql.ResultSet;
import java.sql.SQLException;
import java.util.List;
import java.util.Vector;

import javax.naming.InitialContext;
import javax.sql.DataSource;

public class CountryDerbyDB {

    public CountryDerbyDB() {
    }

    private Connection getConnection() {
        try {
            InitialContext ctx = new InitialContext();
            DataSource ds = (DataSource) ctx.lookup("java:comp/env/jdbc/
                                                CountryDataSource");
            Connection con = ds.getConnection();
            return con;
        } catch (Exception e) {
            e.printStackTrace();
            return null;
        }
    }
```

```java
   private void closeConnection(Connection con) {
      try {
         con.close();
      } catch (SQLException e) {
         e.printStackTrace();
      }
   }

   public List<List<String>> getCountries(String startLetter) {
      List<List<String>> allCountryData = new Vector<List<String>>();
      try {
         Connection con = getConnection();
         PreparedStatement pstmt = con
               .prepareStatement("select short_name,long_
                              name,code,capital,notes from
                               country_data where short_name like
                                                           ?");
         pstmt.setString(1, startLetter + "%");
         ResultSet rs = pstmt.executeQuery();
         while (rs.next()) {
            List<String> countryData = new Vector<String>();
            for (int i = 1; i <= 5; i++) {
               if (i == 5) {
                  String notes = rs.getString(i);
                  if (notes.length() == 0) {
                     notes = " ";
                  }
                  countryData.add(notes);
               } else {
                  countryData.add(rs.getString(i));
               }
            }
            allCountryData.add(countryData);
         }
         rs.close();
         pstmt.close();
      } catch (Exception e) {
         e.printStackTrace();
      }
      finally {
         closeConnection(con);
      }
      return allCountryData;
   }
```

```java
public String[] getCountryData(String ccode) {
   List<String> countryData = new Vector<String>();
   Connection con = getConnection();
   try {
      PreparedStatement pstmt = con
            .prepareStatement("select short_name,long_
                              name,code,capital,notes from
                              country_data where code=?");
      pstmt.setString(1, ccode);
      ResultSet rs = pstmt.executeQuery();
      if (rs.next()) {
         for (int i = 1; i <= 5; i++) {
            if (i == 5) {
               String notes = rs.getString(i);
               if (notes.length() == 0) {
                  notes = " ";
               }
               countryData.add(notes);
            } else {
               countryData.add(rs.getString(i));
            }
         }

      }
   } catch (SQLException e) {
      e.printStackTrace();
   }
   closeConnection(con);
   String[] cdata = new String[5];
   return countryData.toArray(cdata);
}

public String[] saveCountryNotes(String ccode, String notes) {

   Connection con = getConnection();
   try {
      PreparedStatement pstmt = con
            .prepareStatement("update country_data set notes=?
                                                where code=?");
      pstmt.setString(1, notes);
      pstmt.setString(2, ccode);
      pstmt.executeUpdate();
   } catch (SQLException e) {
      e.printStackTrace();
   }
   closeConnection(con);
```

```
            String[] rv = new String[2];
            rv[0] = ccode;
            rv[1] = notes;
            return rv;
        }
}
```

This class has the same methods as the class that used a CSV file as the data source. Note that it would be good to define an interface for similar classes and then use, for example, a factory class to select the correct implementation during run time.

The getConnection() method retrieves a connection from the Geronimo runtime using the specified data source name, and the closeConnection() method closes the connection (or returns it to the Geronimo pool).

The other methods in the class that retrieve or update countries in the database are the ones using plain and simple JDBC calls and SQL scripts.

In order to use this class in our application, we need to configure it to access the **Geronimo Database Pools**. For this, we add data source entries to web.xml and geronimo-web.xml. In the geronimo-web.xml file, we map the database pool that we created earlier to a data source we have specified in the web.xml file.

The following entry in the geronimo-web.xml file configures our database pool as a dependency for our application:

```
<sys:dependencies>
  .
  .
<sys:dependency>
    <sys:groupId>console.dbpool</sys:groupId>
    <sys:artifactId>EasyAjaxDBPool</sys:artifactId>
    <sys:version>1.0</sys:version>
    <sys:type>rar</sys:type>
</sys:dependency>
  .
  .
</sys:dependencies>
```

Moreover, in geronimo-web.xml, there is an entry for mapping a data source name to the database pool. The following entry is just after the context-root element in the XML file.

```
<resource-ref>
    <ref-name>jdbc/CountryDataSource</ref-name>
    <resource-link>EasyAjaxDBPool</resource-link>
</resource-ref>
```

The next configuration for this example is in the web.xml file, where we set up a resource reference so that our classes can use it. The following entry is at the end of the web.xml file.

```
<resource-ref>
  <res-ref-name>jdbc/CountryDataSource</res-ref-name>
  <res-type>javax.sql.DataSource</res-type>
  <res-auth>Container</res-auth>
  <res-sharing-scope>Shareable</res-sharing-scope>
</resource-ref>
```

And finally, the last configuration we do here is to change the remoted class in the dwr.xml file to the new CountryDerbyDB class. In the DWR configuration, we change the class parameter for CountryDB.

```
<create creator="new" javascript="CountryDB">
  <param name="class" value="samples.CountryDerbyDB" />
  <include method="getCountries" />
  <include method="saveCountryNotes" />
  <include method="getCountryData" />
</create>
```

Testing the Database Integration

We verify whether this works by changing the notes of some country and then checking that these notes were saved to the database. In this example, we change the note for The Bahamas and then, using the **Geronimo Console**, we check that the notes for The Bahamas were indeed stored to the database as shown in the following screenshot:

DB Viewer					help [view]

DB: EasyAjaxDatabase   Table: APP.COUNTRY_DATA

ID	SHORT_NAME	LONG_NAME	CODE	CAPITAL	NOTES
1	Afghanistan	Islamic Republic of Afghanistan	AF	Kabul	
2	Albania	Republic of Albania	AL	Tirana	
3	Algeria	Peoples Democratic Republic of Algeria	AG	Algiers	
4	Andorra	Principality of Andorra	AN	Andorra la Vella	
5	Angola	Republic of Angola	AO	Luanda	
6	Antigua andBarbuda	(no long-form name)	AC	Saint Johns	
7	Argentina	Argentine Republic	AR	Buenos Aires	
8	Armenia	Republic of Armenia	AM	Yerevan	
9	Australia	Commonwealth of Australia	AS	Canberra	
10	Austria	Republic of Austria	AU	Vienna	
11	Azerbaijan	Republic of Azerbaijan	AJ	Baku	
12	Bahamas	The Commonwealth of The Bahamas	BF	Nassau	In the Caribbean
13	Bahrain	Kingdom of Bahrain	BA	Manama	
14	Bangladesh	Peoples Republicof Bangladesh	BG	Dhaka	
15	Barbados	(no long-form name)	BB	Bridgetown	
16	Belarus	Republic of Belarus	BO	Minsk	
17	Belgium	Kingdom of Belgium	BE	Brussels	

Afterword

Database integration is very easy to achieve and, in fact does not affect the DWR functionality in any way. Accessing the database uses just another Java class, and if we remote it, we can use DWR to access it from the browser.

Integrating with Web Services

In this chapter, we use a third-party web service to do the credit card validation. This credit card validation service was found (after a quick search) on the Internet, and it is suitable for our example. The web service is hosted by a company called Hypercom (http://www.hypercom.com).

Developing the Web Service Client

The service is a standard web service with a WSDL description, which makes it easy for us to integrate it into our application. The WSDL is located at `http://www.tpisoft.com/smartpayments/validate.asmx?WSDL`. As is apparent from the URL, the service is not Java based. In the web services world, the implementation does not matter as long as the interfaces are standard.

We use built-in tools of Eclipse to generate client-side code for the credit card validator web service.

1. Web services are created using wizards in the Eclipse IDE. Select project **DWREasyAjax**, and in the **File | New | Other** menu, there is a wizard to create the **Web Service Client**.

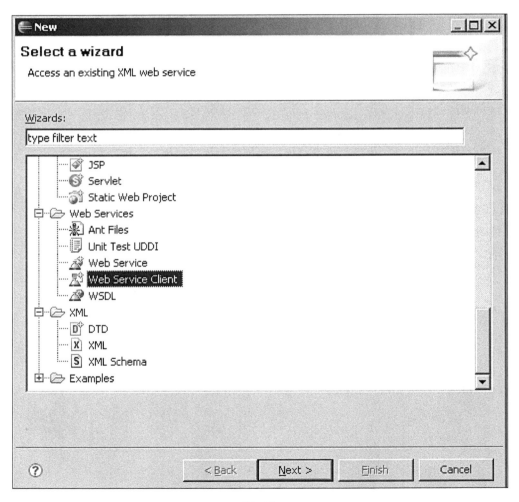

2. Clicking the **Next** button opens up the next screen of the wizard where we select the WSDL file for the client and decide whether we want to assemble, test, or just develop the client. We choose to develop the client since testing will be done by our application.

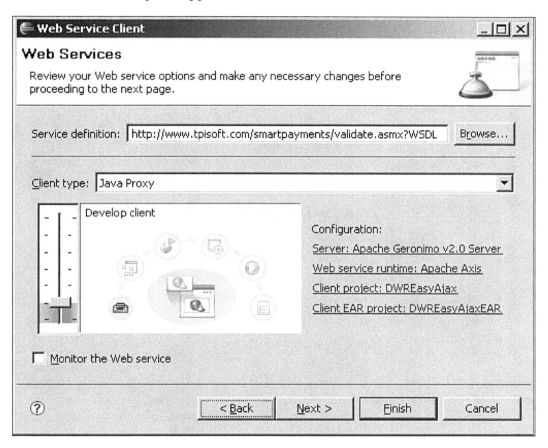

3. The service definition has the WSDL URL. We can leave the other settings at their defaults; pressing **Finish** will generate classes for the **Web Service Client.**

After a brief moment, client classes for the **CreditCardValidator** web service are created by Eclipse. The default location is our project's **source** directory. The following screenshot shows the generated classes:

There are just a couple of classes that we need: CreditCardValidatorSoap, which is actually an interface and used indirectly, and CreditCardValidatorSoapProxy, which is responsible for instantiating the implementation class of the CreditCardValidatorSoap interface and acting as proxy to the implementation class. The following is the source code for the CreditCardValidatorSoap interface. This interface is automatically generated from WSDL, and because the WSDL file included the documentation for web service operations, Eclipse tooling also provides the documentation for the generated methods as shown here:

```
/**
 * CreditCardValidatorSoap.java
 *
 * This file was auto-generated from WSDL
 * by the Apache Axis 1.4 Apr 22, 2006 (06:55:48 PDT) WSDL2Java
emitter.
 */
```

```java
package localhost.SmartPayments;

public interface CreditCardValidatorSoap extends java.rmi.Remote {

    /**
     * Returns the card issuer Visa, MasterCard, AMEX, etc., based
     * on the card number.
     */
    public java.lang.String getCardType(java.lang.String cardNumber)
                            throws java.rmi.RemoteException;

    /**
     * Returns (T/F) if the card is a known commercial card
(commercial
     * cards require customer code and sales tax amount to receive
                                                        preferred
     * discount rate pricing.)
     */
    public boolean isCommercialCard(java.lang.String cardNumber)
                            throws java.rmi.RemoteException;

    /**
     * Validates the credit card by checking the card length based
     * on the card type, performs a mod 10 checksum and validates the
expiration
     * date. Returns 0 if good, 1001 - no card number, 1002 - no exp
                                                            date,
     * 1003 - invalid card type, 1004 - invalid card length,
                                                1005 - bad mod
     * 10 check, 1006 - bad expiration date.
     */
    public int validCard(java.lang.String cardNumber, java.lang.String
                        expDate) throws java.rmi.RemoteException;

    /**
     * Validates the credit card length by checking the card length
     * based on the card type, Returns (T/F).
     */
    public boolean validCardLength(java.lang.String cardNumber)
                            throws java.rmi.RemoteException;

    /**
     * Validates the expiration date by making sure it is a valid
     * date and the card has not expired, Returns (T/F).
     */
    public boolean validExpDate(java.lang.String expDate)
                            throws java.rmi.RemoteException;
```

```
/**
 * Validates the credit card by performing a mod 10 checksum on
 * the card number, Returns (T/F).
 */
public boolean validMod10(java.lang.String cardNumber)
                              throws java.rmi.RemoteException;

/**
 * Lookup the Debit Network ID using a Card Number. Network ID
 * is a 3 characters string. If there is a match, the card can
likely
 * be used as a Debit Card and processed through the Debit
network. Possible
 * Network ID: ACL â€" Accel, AFN - AFFN, AKO â€" Alaska Option,
C24 â€" CU24,
 * ILK â€" Interlink, JEN - Jeanie, MAC â€" Star Northeast (MAC),
MAE â€" Maestro,
 * NET - NETS, NYC â€" NYCE, PUL â€" Pulse, SES â€" Star
Southeast, SHZ â€" Shazam,
 * STX â€" Star West, TYM - TYME
 */
public localhost.SmartPayments.Response getNetworkID(java.
lang.String userName, java.lang.String password, java.lang.String
cardNumber) throws java.rmi.RemoteException;
}
```

There are several methods defined in the class, but we use only the `validCard()` method, which returns 0 if the credit card is valid.

The source code for the `CreditCardValidatorSoapProxy` class is explained in the following snippet. This class implements the the `CreditCardValidatorSoap` interface.

The source code of `CreditCardValidatorSoapProxy` is shown here for example purposes, so we can really appreciate the tooling that is provided by Eclipse. Developing web services clients manually would mean quite a lot of coding and understanding of SOAP and other related web service standards, but since Eclipse has the tools to generate the necessary implementation classes from the WSDL, we don't really have to worry about SOAP details or other web services "stuff" (other than how to use the client, of course).

```
package localhost.SmartPayments;

public class CreditCardValidatorSoapProxy implements localhost.
SmartPayments.CreditCardValidatorSoap {
  private String _endpoint = null;
```

```
private localhost.SmartPayments.CreditCardValidatorSoap
                          creditCardValidatorSoap = null;

public CreditCardValidatorSoapProxy() {
  _initCreditCardValidatorSoapProxy();
}

public CreditCardValidatorSoapProxy(String endpoint) {
  _endpoint = endpoint;
  _initCreditCardValidatorSoapProxy();
}

private void _initCreditCardValidatorSoapProxy() {
  try {
    creditCardValidatorSoap = (new localhost.SmartPayments.
                          CreditCardValidatorLocator()).
                            getCreditCardValidatorSoap();
    if (creditCardValidatorSoap != null) {
      if (_endpoint != null)
        ((javax.xml.rpc.Stub)creditCardValidatorSoap)._
          setProperty("javax.xml.rpc.service.endpoint.address",
                                              _endpoint);
      else
        _endpoint = (String)((javax.xml.rpc.Stub)
                          creditCardValidatorSoap).
                            _getProperty("javax.xml.rpc.service.
                                      endpoint.address");
    }

  }
  catch (javax.xml.rpc.ServiceException serviceException) {}
}

public String getEndpoint() {
  return _endpoint;
}

public void setEndpoint(String endpoint) {
  _endpoint = endpoint;
  if (creditCardValidatorSoap != null)
    ((javax.xml.rpc.Stub)creditCardValidatorSoap)._
      setProperty("javax.xml.rpc.service.endpoint.address",
                                        _endpoint);

}
```

```java
  public localhost.SmartPayments.CreditCardValidatorSoap
getCreditCardValidatorSoap() {
    if (creditCardValidatorSoap == null)
      _initCreditCardValidatorSoapProxy();
    return creditCardValidatorSoap;
  }


  public java.lang.String getCardType(java.lang.String cardNumber)
throws java.rmi.RemoteException{
    if (creditCardValidatorSoap == null)
      _initCreditCardValidatorSoapProxy();
    return creditCardValidatorSoap.getCardType(cardNumber);
  }


  public boolean isCommercialCard(java.lang.String cardNumber) throws
   java.rmi.RemoteException{
    if (creditCardValidatorSoap == null)
      _initCreditCardValidatorSoapProxy();
    return creditCardValidatorSoap.isCommercialCard(cardNumber);
  }


  public int validCard(java.lang.String cardNumber, java.lang.String
                       expDate) throws java.rmi.RemoteException{
    if (creditCardValidatorSoap == null)
      _initCreditCardValidatorSoapProxy();
    return creditCardValidatorSoap.validCard(cardNumber, expDate);
  }


  public boolean validCardLength(java.lang.String cardNumber) throws
   java.rmi.RemoteException{
    if (creditCardValidatorSoap == null)
      _initCreditCardValidatorSoapProxy();
    return creditCardValidatorSoap.validCardLength(cardNumber);
  }


  public boolean validExpDate(java.lang.String expDate) throws java.
   rmi.RemoteException{
    if (creditCardValidatorSoap == null)
      _initCreditCardValidatorSoapProxy();
    return creditCardValidatorSoap.validExpDate(expDate);
  }


  public boolean validMod10(java.lang.String cardNumber) throws java.
   rmi.RemoteException{
```

```
      if (creditCardValidatorSoap == null)
        _initCreditCardValidatorSoapProxy();
      return creditCardValidatorSoap.validMod10(cardNumber);
    }

    public localhost.SmartPayments.Response getNetworkID
      (java.lang.String userName, java.lang.String password,
        java.lang.String cardNumber) throws java.rmi.RemoteException{
      if (creditCardValidatorSoap == null)
        _initCreditCardValidatorSoapProxy();
      return creditCardValidatorSoap.getNetworkID(userName, password,
                                                     cardNumber);
    }
  }
```

The above proxy class is automatically generated by Eclipse tooling, and in most cases, knowledge of the details of the generated classes is not needed. The proxy class basically initializes yet another automatically generated class for the CreditCardValidatorSoap interface that has the code to actually call a remote web service.

Implementing the Web Service Call

The CreditCardValidatorSoapProxy class will be used in our example. We modify the FormHandler class and replace the implementation of the submitOrder() method with the following code:

```
public boolean submitOrder(String name, String address,
        String creditCardNumber, String expiryDate) {
    CreditCardValidatorSoapProxy ccValidatorProxy = new
CreditCardValidatorSoapProxy();
    int rv = -1;
    try {
        rv = ccValidatorProxy.validCard(creditCardNumber,
                                        expiryDate.replace("/",
                                                            ""));
        if (rv != 0) {
            System.out.println("Credit card check failed: " + rv);
        }
    } catch (RemoteException e) {
        e.printStackTrace();
    }
    return rv == 0;
}
```

In the above method, we first instantiate the `CreditCardValidatorSoapProxy` object and then call its `validCard()` method to do the credit card validation. The `validCard()` method calls the remote web service via Internet. If the credit card is not valid, a notification is written to the `System.out`, and the `submitOrder()` method returns `false`. If the credit card is valid, then the `submitOrder()` method returns `true`.

Using the existing tools in Eclipse and just a couple of lines of code, we can integrate standard web services into our example.

Testing Web Services Integration

We test the web services integration using the form example. Since we have just updated the form example to use a web service for credit card validation we can verify whether a web service is called using, for example, the Wireshark network protocol analyzer (`http://www.wireshark.org`), or the TCP/IP monitor that comes with Eclipse tooling. The following is a screenshot of a web service request from Geronimo to a web service provider:

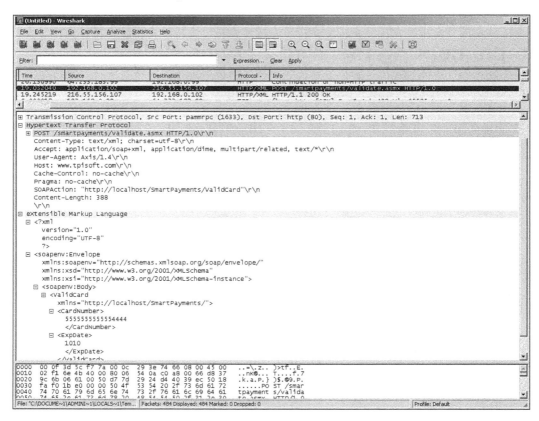

The response from the web service is also captured by Wireshark. The following is a screenshot of the response:

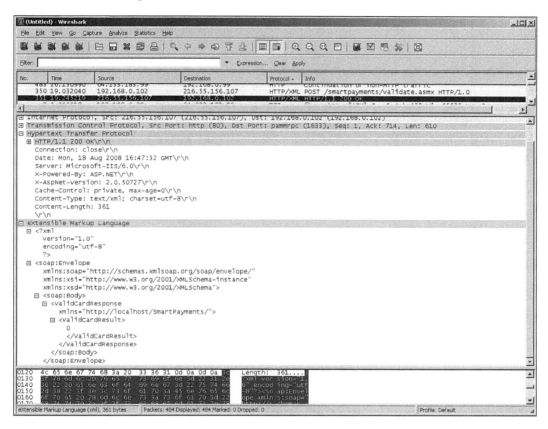

Afterword

Web service integration is just as easy as the database integration shown in the previous section. Again, DWR and the user interface do not know the implementation of the remote Java classes, so the web service integration is very transparent to users.

Integrating with a Messaging System

The idea behind the messaging example is that our application will send an order form to the backend system using JMS. The backend system here is a Python script that accesses the JMS messaging server, ActiveMQ.

Setting up Queues in Geronimo

In this messaging example, we use an open-source JMS messaging server, ActiveMQ, that is a part of the Geronimo application server. ActiveMQ is very good for testing our application since it supports a protocol called **STOMP (Streaming Text Oriented Messaging Protocol**, a text based protocol). STOMP enables many kinds of programming languages to participate in JMS messaging (even Telnet is possible; useful for quick testing) so we can use the existing tool as our "order system" in our example. When the "order system" (a Python program) receives the order it verifies it. Then, we manually send an order confirmation message back to the ActiveMQ messaging system and to our application. Then our application updates the web page using the **Comet** mechanism.

1. The first thing to do is to create queues in the ActiveMQ for sending orders and receiving order confirmations. We use wizards in the **Geronimo Server Console** to create queues. JMS resources are found in the console **Services | JMS Resources**.

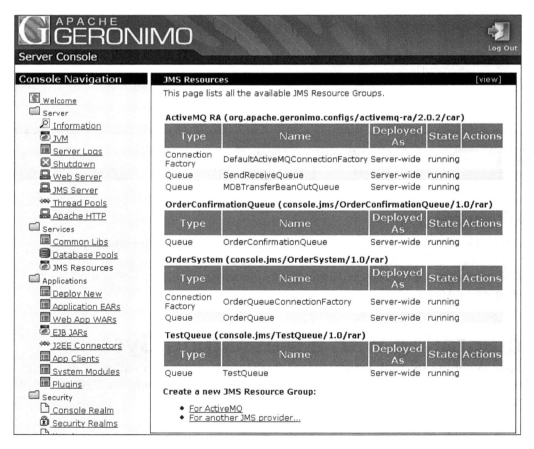

2. In order to create a new queue, we set up a new resource by clicking (**Create a new JMS Resource Group**) **For ActiveMQ link**. The link opens a wizard to create a new resource group as shown in the following screenshot:

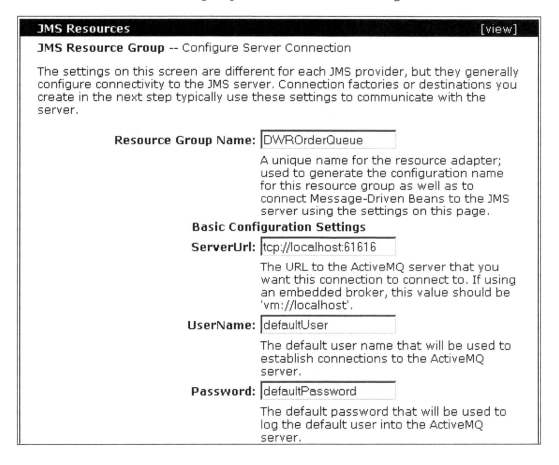

3. We only need to set a name for the resource group. We use the name **DWROrderQueue** as the queue name for submitting orders. All other configuration entries can be left to default values. Clicking the **Next** button opens a screen as shown next:

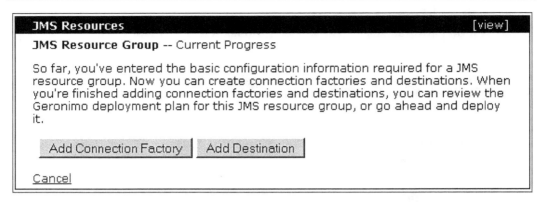

4. We want to set up a new destination, so clicking the **Add Destination** button opens the screen to **Select Destination Type**.

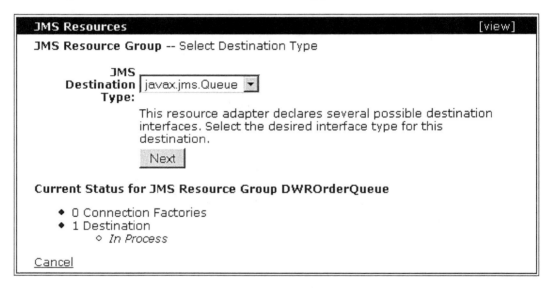

5. We use **Queue** as destination, and in the next screen, we configure the **Destination Name** and **PhysicalName** for the queue. Both are named DWROrderQueue.

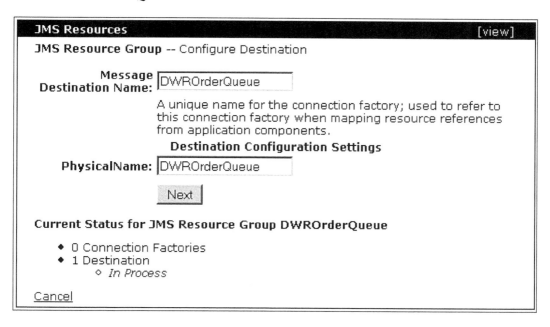

6. Clicking on the **Next** button opens a summary screen showing what we have created so far.

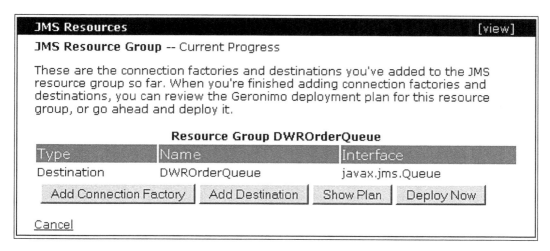

7. Here, we can **Add Destination** or **Add Connection Factory**. The button **Deploy Now** deploys a queue to Geronimo.

8. We also create **DWROrderConfirmationQueue** (similar to steps 1-7), and then we have our queues set up for the example.

DWROrderConfirmationQueue
(console.jms/DWROrderConfirmationQueue/1.0/rar)

Type	Name	Deployed As	State	Actions
Queue	DWROrderConfirmationQueue	Server-wide	running	

DWROrderQueue (console.jms/DWROrderQueue/1.0/rar)

Type	Name	Deployed As	State	Actions
Queue	DWROrderQueue	Server-wide	running	

Developing the OrderSystem Java Class

The next step is to create a class to call our "order system". Because asynchronous messaging is used, the class will be started in a thread during order submission. The OrderSystem in our example is a manual process, and the thread will wait for the confirmation message and will then use reverse AJAX to update the web page.

The following is the source code for the OrderSystem class:

```
package samples;

import java.util.Collection;
import java.util.Iterator;
import java.util.Properties;

import javax.jms.Connection;
import javax.jms.ConnectionFactory;
import javax.jms.DeliveryMode;
import javax.jms.Destination;
import javax.jms.MessageConsumer;
import javax.jms.MessageProducer;
import javax.jms.Session;
import javax.jms.TextMessage;
import javax.naming.Context;
import javax.naming.InitialContext;
import javax.servlet.ServletContext;

import org.directwebremoting.ScriptBuffer;
import org.directwebremoting.ScriptSession;
import org.directwebremoting.ServerContext;
```

```
import org.directwebremoting.ServerContextFactory;
import org.directwebremoting.WebContext;
import org.directwebremoting.WebContextFactory;

public class OrderSystem implements Runnable {
    protected Thread worker;
    private ServerContext serverContext;
    private String scriptId = null;
    private String name;
    private String address;
    private String creditCardNumber;
    private String expiryDate;

    public OrderSystem(String name, String address,
                       String creditCardNumber,
                                    String expiryDate) {
        this.name = name;
        this.address = address;
        this.creditCardNumber = creditCardNumber;
        this.expiryDate = expiryDate;
        WebContext webContext = WebContextFactory.get();
        ServletContext servletContext = webContext.getServletContext();

        serverContext = ServerContextFactory.get(servletContext);

        // A bit nasty: the call to serverContext.
          getScriptSessionsByPage()
        // below could fail because the system might need to read
                                                web.xml which
        // means it needs a ServletContext, which is only available
            using
        // WebContext, which in turn requires a DWR thread. We can cache
            the
        // results simply by calling this in a DWR thread, as we are
            now.
        webContext.getScriptSessionsByPage("");

        scriptId = webContext.getScriptSession().getId();
        worker = new Thread(this, "OrderSystem");
        worker.start();
    }

    public void run() {
        String returnFromOrderSystem = "";
        try {
            Properties props = new Properties();
            props.setProperty(Context.INITIAL_CONTEXT_FACTORY,
```

```
                "org.apache.activemq.jndi.ActiveMQInitialContextFactory");
        props.setProperty(Context.PROVIDER_URL,
                        "tcp://localhost:61616");
        props.setProperty("queue.DWROrderQueue", "DWROrderQueue");
        props.setProperty("queue.DWROrderConfirmationQueue",
            "DWROrderConfirmationQueue");
        javax.naming.Context ctx = new InitialContext(props);
        ConnectionFactory connectionFactory = (ConnectionFactory) ctx
            .lookup("ConnectionFactory");
        Connection connection = connectionFactory.createConnection();
        connection.start();

        Session session = connection.createSession(false,
            Session.AUTO_ACKNOWLEDGE);
        Destination destination = (Destination)
                        ctx.lookup("DWROrderQueue");
        MessageProducer producer =
                        session.createProducer(destination);
        producer.setDeliveryMode(DeliveryMode.NON_PERSISTENT);

        String orderMessage = "Order from: " + name + ",
                        " + address + ","
            + creditCardNumber + "," + expiryDate
            + ". Please return order ID.";
        String receiverQName = "DWROrderConfirmationQueue";
        orderMessage = "ReceiverQueue: " + receiverQName + "||   "
            + orderMessage;
        TextMessage message = session.createTextMessage(orderMessage
);
        producer.send(message);
        Destination receiveDestination = (Destination) ctx
            .lookup(receiverQName);
        MessageConsumer consumer = session
            .createConsumer(receiveDestination);
        TextMessage returnMessage = (TextMessage)
                        consumer.receive(60000);
        if (returnMessage == null) {
            returnFromOrderSystem = "<p><font color=\"red\">Order
confirmation not received. Please contact administrator.</font></p>";
        } else {
            returnFromOrderSystem = "<p><font color=\"green\">Order
                        confirmation received. Order ID: "
            + returnMessage.getText() + ".</font></p>";
        }
        session.close();
        connection.close();
```

```
        } catch (Exception e) {
            e.printStackTrace();
        }
        Collection<ScriptSession> sessions = serverContext
                .getAllScriptSessions();
        for (Iterator<ScriptSession> iterator = sessions.iterator();
                                                    iterator
                .hasNext();) {
            ScriptSession scriptSession = iterator.next();
            if (scriptSession.getId().equals(scriptId)) {
                ScriptBuffer script = new ScriptBuffer("orderProcessed('"
                        + returnFromOrderSystem + "')");
                scriptSession.addScript(script);
            }
        }
    }
}
```

This class uses DWR reverse AJAX functionality. What is interesting about reverse AJAX here is that it is used from a non-web thread. In this case, when submitting the order, a new thread is started that sends a message via JMS to OrderSystem and waits for the response. When the response comes, or a timeout occurs, DWR methods are used to send a message to the web page.

The constructor of the OrderSystem class uses the DWR functionality to get web context for the calling web page. The code is provided by DWR and, as the comment in the source code indicates, it is little "hacky". At the end of the constructor, we get the script session ID of a calling page so we may send a response back to the correct web page and the orderProcessed() function can process the response in the index.jsp file. And finally, the constructor starts the worker thread and returns control to the calling method.

The run() method first initializes the JNDI initial context and then starts the JMS connection to the local ActiveMQ. Standard JMS methods are used to send order messages and then wait for responses to arrive in DWROrderConfirmationQueue.

Setting up the Application for Messaging

In this section, we set up our example application for messaging by developing JavaScript functions and a Java class for submitting orders. We also set up reverse AJAX in this section.

The JavaScript function to receive order confirmation in the web page is as follows and we add it to `index.jsp` together with most of the other JavaScript functions.

```
function orderProcessed(orderConfirmationMessage)
{
    var feedback=dwr.util.byId('formFeedback');
    var html="";
    html=orderConfirmationMessage;
    feedback.innerHTML=html;
}
```

In order to integrate the order system with the submission process, we change the code for the `submitOrder()` method in the `FormHandler` class. The new code for this method is as follows:

```
public boolean submitOrder(String name, String address,
        String creditCardNumber, String expiryDate) {
    CreditCardValidatorSoapProxy ccValidatorProxy = new
CreditCardValidatorSoapProxy();
    int rv = -1;
    try {
        rv = ccValidatorProxy.validCard(creditCardNumber,
                                    expiryDate.replace("/", ""));
        if (rv != 0) {
            System.out.println("Credit card check failed: " + rv);
        }
    } catch (RemoteException e) {
        e.printStackTrace();
    }
    if(rv==0)
    {
        //credit card valid, submit to order system
        new OrderSystem(name,address,creditCardNumber,expiryDate);
    }
    return rv == 0;
}
```

The new addition here is after the web service call to the `CreditCardValidator` (shown in bold in the previous code). If the credit card is valid, then the `OrderSystem` class is instantiated. Because it has a constructor that starts a new thread for processing, there is no need for any variables. When the thread completes, there will be no references to the `OrderSystem` class, and Java's garbage collector will clean up leftover objects.

The next step is to enable reverse AJAX for DWR, which is very simple. We just add the following `init` parameter to the `web.xml` file.

```
<init-param>
  <param-name>activeReverseAjaxEnabled</param-name>
  <param-value>true</param-value>
</init-param>
```

We also enable reverse AJAX for our application in the `index.jsp` page. Add the following line to the `loadMenuItems()` function in the `index.jsp` file.

```
dwr.engine.setActiveReverseAjax(true);
```

Testing with the Backend OrderSystem

Our "order system" is a Python-based STOMP client for Active MQ. The Python client is called `stomp.py`, and it is a open-source library by Jason Briggs (`http://www.briggs.net.nz/log/projects/stomppy/`). Python itself can be downloaded and installed from `http://www.python.org`. The Python version 2.5.1 is used in this example:

1. Testing messaging is done by starting the "order system" using the command **python stomp.py localhost 61613** in the directory, where `stomp.py` is located. The command connects to `ActiveMQ` and opens a session.

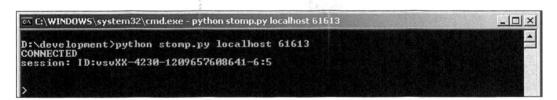

2. We subscribe to `DWROrderQueue` using the **subscribe /queue/ DWROrderQueue.** command.

3. Now the "order system" waits for orders, and we can use a web application to submit the order. After the order has been submitted, the ActiveMQ JMS provider sends a message to the order queue, and because we subscribed the stomp client to receive the order messages, we get the message in our "order system".

4. We have one minute before a timeout occurs in the web client, so we quickly send the order confirmation to DWROrderConfirmationQueue using the **send** /queue/DWROrderConfirmationQueue 1234567890ABCDEF command.

5. We get the order confirmation back to the web application as is shown in the following screenshot:

Afterword

Using messaging in a DWR application is easy, just like using a database or web services. In this case, messaging gives a good channel for a platform to communicate directly with the user when using reverse AJAX.

Summary

We had three examples for backend integration in this chapter: database, web services, and messaging. One or more of these are found in almost all applications, and as the examples presented, DWR is agnostic to backend integration. It is possible to use the most familiar technology to access databases and other backend services and let DWR handle only the frontend user interface.

We also saw how Comet technology is used in the DWR messaging example, where Comet is a natural fit, by providing event-style messaging between the browser and the server.

7
Sample Applications

This chapter includes two sample applications that use some of the functionalities that were presented in the samples in the previous chapters. The first sample application is Collaborative Book Authoring, which enables multiple users to author the same book. The second sample application is a straightforward chat room application.

These samples concentrate on the DWR functionality, which means that much of the features of real production-grade applications are missing from the sample applications. However, the samples show how DWR is used, and it should be easy to enhance applications to production grade using the samples as a starting point for development and as a source of ideas.

Two sample applications in this chapter are as follows:

- Collaborative Book Authoring—shows how DWR is used to create a web-based, multi-user authoring environment
- Chatroom—a typical multi-user chat room application using DWR

Collaborative Book Authoring

The Collaborative Book Authoring sample application enables multiple users to work on the same or different books simultaneously. The idea is that an author logs into a system and he/she sees all the books that are in process, and have been published. Anyone can start a new book and anyone can contribute to a book (so this is quite an open process). Also within a book, anyone can start a new chapter and again anyone can edit the chapter content. The system is built so that only one author can edit a chapter. If someone is editing a chapter content, and another user tries to edit it, he/she will see the most recent save of the chapter content.

When the book is finished, authors will vote for publishing. Authors can vote only once, and a vote cannot be taken back. When all the authors have voted for publishing, the book is moved to a published status, and it is formatted for reading.

Starting the Project

We start the project by creating a new web project in Eclipse using the name **DWRBookAuthoring**. In this case, development starts with the HTML pages. We need a login page, login failed page, and main page that will hold all the JavaScript functions. We will also use the CSS from the Dynamic Drive as we did in the previous chapters.

The following screenshot shows what kind of user interface we are developing:

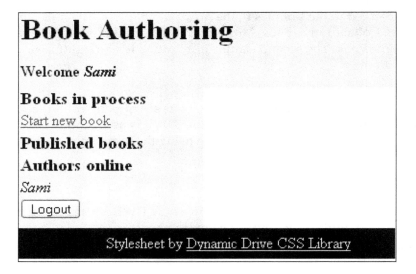

Developing the User Interface

We start the application development with the user interface. First, we get the style sheet. The source code of the style sheet is given next. Just like the style sheets in the previous chapters, this CSS is also from the Dynamic Drive CSS library, `http://www.dynamicdrive.com/style/`.

```
body{
margin:0;
padding:0;
line-height: 1.5em;
}
```

```
b{font-size: 110%;}
em{color: red;}

#topsection{
background: #EAEAEA;
height: 90px; /*Height of top section*/
}

#topsection h1{
margin: 0;
padding-top: 15px;
}

#contentwrapper{
float: left;
width: 100%;
}

#contentcolumn{
margin-left: 200px; /*Set left margin to LeftColumnWidth*/
}

#leftcolumn{
float: left;
width: 200px; /*Width of left column*/
margin-left: -100%;
background: #C8FC98;
}

#footer{
clear: left;
width: 100%;
background: black;
color: #FFF;
text-align: center;
padding: 4px 0;
}

#footer a{
color: #FFFF80;
}

.innertube{
margin: 10px; /*Margins for inner DIV inside each column (to provide
padding)*/
margin-top: 0;
}
```

index.jsp

Our first page is the login page. It is located in the **WebContent** directory and it is named `index.jsp`. The source code for the page is given here (incidentally, the login page does not use the style sheet).

```jsp
<%@ page language="java" contentType="text/html; charset=ISO-8859-1"
    pageEncoding="ISO-8859-1"%>
<!DOCTYPE html PUBLIC "-//W3C//DTD HTML 4.01 Transitional//EN"
"http://www.w3.org/TR/html4/loose.dtd">
<html>
<head>
<meta http-equiv="Content-Type" content="text/html; charset=ISO-8859-
1">
<title>Book Authoring</title>

<script type='text/javascript' src='/DWRBookAuthoring/dwr/interface/
Login.js'></script>
<script type='text/javascript' src='/DWRBookAuthoring/dwr/engine.
js'></script>
<script type='text/javascript' src='/DWRBookAuthoring/dwr/util.js'>
                                                        </script>

<script type="text/javascript">

function login()
{
  var userNameInput=dwr.util.byId('userName');
  var userName=userNameInput.value;
  Login.doLogin(userName,loginResult);
}

function loginResult(newPage)
{
  window.location.href=newPage;
}

</script>
</head>
<body>
<h1>Book Authoring Sample</h1>
<table cellpadding="0" cellspacing="0">
<tr>
<td>User name:</td>
<td><input id="userName" type="text" size="30"></td>
</tr>
<tr>
<td> </td>
<td><input type="button" value="Login" onclick="login();return
false;"></td>
</tr></table>
</body>
</html>
```

The login screen uses the DWR functionality to process the user login (the Java classes are presented after the web pages). The `loginResults` function opens either the failure page or the main page based on the result of the login operation.

loginFailed.html

If the login was unsuccessful, a very simple `loginFailed.html` page is shown to the user, the source code for which is as follows:

```
<!DOCTYPE html PUBLIC "-//W3C//DTD HTML 4.01 Transitional//EN"
 "http://www.w3.org/TR/html4/loose.dtd">
<html>
<head>
<meta http-equiv="Content-Type" content="text/html;
 charset=ISO-8859-1">
<title>Login failed</title>
</head>
<body>
<h2>Login failed.</h2>
</body>
</html>
```

mainpage.jsp

If the login was successful, we get the main page, `mainpage.jsp`:

```
<!DOCTYPE html PUBLIC "-//W3C//DTD XHTML 1.0 Transitional//EN"
"http://www.w3.org/TR/xhtml1/DTD/xhtml1-transitional.dtd">
<html xmlns="http://www.w3.org/1999/xhtml" lang="en" xml:lang="en">
<head>
<meta http-equiv="Content-Type" content="text/html;
 charset=iso-8859-1" />
<title>Book Authoring</title>
<link href="styles.css" rel="stylesheet" type="text/css" />
<%
    if (session.getAttribute("username") == null
         || session.getAttribute("username").equals("")) {
      //if not logged in and trying to access this page
      //do nothing, browser shows empty page
      return;
    }
%>
<script type='text/javascript'
  src='/DWRBookAuthoring/dwr/interface/Login.js'></script>
<script type='text/javascript'
```

```
    src='/DWRBookAuthoring/dwr/interface/BookDatabase.js'></script>
<script type='text/javascript'
    src='/DWRBookAuthoring/dwr/engine.js'></script>
<script type='text/javascript' src='/DWRBookAuthoring/dwr/util.js'>
                                                            </script>

<script type="text/javascript">
dwr.engine.setActiveReverseAjax(true);

function logout()
{
  Login.doLogout(showLoginScreen);
}

function showLoginScreen()
{
  window.location.href='index.jsp';
}

function showUsersOnline()
{
  var cellFuncs = [
          function(author) {

              return '<i>'+author+'</i>';
          }
          ];
      Login.getUsersOnline({
      callback:function(authors)
      {
        dwr.util.removeAllRows('authorsOnline');
        dwr.util.addRows( "authorsOnline",authors, cellFuncs,
                        { escapeHtml:false });
      }
      });
}

function getBookLists()
{
  var cellFuncs = [
          function(title) {

              return '<a href="#" onclick="getChapters(this);">'+title+
                                                            '</a>';
          }
          ];
```

```
    BookDatabase.getBooksInProgressTitles({
    callback:function(titles)
    {
      dwr.util.removeAllRows('booksInProgress');
      dwr.util.addRows( "booksInProgress",titles , cellFuncs,
                  { escapeHtml:false });
    }
    });

    var cellFuncs2 = [
         function(title) {

            return '<a href="#" onclick="showBook(this);">'+title+'
                                                       </a>';
         }
         ];
    BookDatabase.getPublishedBookTitles({
    callback:function(titles)
    {
      dwr.util.removeAllRows('publishedBooks');
      dwr.util.addRows( "publishedBooks",titles , cellFuncs2,
                  { escapeHtml:false });
    }
    });
}

function getChapters(element)
{
  var bookTitle=element.firstChild.nodeValue;
  getChaptersForTitle(bookTitle);
}

function showBook(element)
{
  var bookTitle=element.firstChild.nodeValue;
  BookDatabase.getRenderedBook(bookTitle,{
         callback:function(bookContent)
         {
           clearContentAreas();
           //title area is used to show published book
           var contentArea=dwr.util.byId('bookTitleContentArea');
           contentArea.innerHTML=bookContent;
         }
       });
}
```

```
function getChaptersForTitle(bookTitle)
{
    clearContentAreas();
    BookDatabase.getChapters(bookTitle,{
    callback:function(titles)
    {
      var titleArea=dwr.util.byId('bookTitleContentArea');
      var html='<h3>Chapters for <div id="chaptersForTitle"><i>'
                  +bookTitle+'</i></div></h3>';

      BookDatabase.getAuthors(bookTitle,{
          async:false,
          callback:function(authors)
          {
            html+='Authors: '+authors;
          }
        });
      titleArea.innerHTML=html;
      var cellFuncs = [function(title) {

            return '<a href="#" onclick="getChapterContent
            (\''+bookTitle+'\', \''+title+'\');">'+title+'</a>';
          }
          ];
      dwr.util.removeAllRows('bookChapters');
      dwr.util.addRows( "bookChapters",titles , cellFuncs,
                    { escapeHtml:false });
      var insertChapterArea=dwr.util.byId('insertChapterArea');

      var numberOfVotes=0;
       BookDatabase.getNumberOfVotes(bookTitle,{
          async:false,
          callback:function(n)
          {
            numberOfVotes=n;
          }
        });

      var totalNumberOfAuthors=0;
       BookDatabase.getNumberOfAuthors(bookTitle,{
          async:false,
          callback:function(n)
          {
            totalNumberOfAuthors=n;
          }
```

```
        });
      var voteDisabled='';
       BookDatabase.haveIVoted(bookTitle,{
          async:false,
          callback:function(haveIVoted)
          {
            if(haveIVoted==true)
            {
              voteDisabled='DISABLED';
            }
          }
        });

      insertChapterArea.innerHTML='<a href="#" onclick="addChapter
        (\''+bookTitle+'\');">Add new chapter</a>';
       BookDatabase.amIAuthor(bookTitle,{
          async:false,
          callback:function(amIAuthor)
          {
            if(amIAuthor==true)
            {
              var voteArea=dwr.util.byId('voteArea');
              var voteAreaHtml='<input type="button" value="Vote
for publish" '+voteDisabled+' onclick="voteForPublish(\
''+bookTitle+'\');">';;
              voteAreaHtml+='<br/>Total votes: '+numberOfVotes+'
                  /'+totalNumberOfAuthors+'.';
              voteArea.innerHTML=voteAreaHtml;
            }

          }
        });
    }
    });
}

function voteForPublish(bookTitle)
{
    var confirmation=confirm('You can not take back your vote. Are you
                          sure that you want to vote?');
    if(confirmation)
    {   BookDatabase.voteForPublish(bookTitle,{
          callback:function()
          {
            getChaptersForTitle(bookTitle);
```

```
        }
      });
    }
  }

  function refreshChapterIfVisible(bookTitle)
  {
    var chaptersForTitle=dwr.util.byId('chaptersForTitle');
    if(chaptersForTitle!=null || chaptersForTitle!=undefined)
    {
      if(chaptersForTitle.innerHTML.indexOf(bookTitle)>-1)
      {
        getChaptersForTitle(bookTitle);
      }
    }
  }

  function clearChapterViewIfVisible(bookTitle)
  {
    var chaptersForTitle=dwr.util.byId('chaptersForTitle');
    if(chaptersForTitle!=null || chaptersForTitle!=undefined)
    {
      if(chaptersForTitle.innerHTML.indexOf(bookTitle)>-1)
      {
        clearContentAreas();
      }
    }
  }

  function notifyBookPublished(bookTitle)
  {
    alert('Book '+bookTitle+' is published. Authors have voted.');
    clearChapterViewIfVisible(bookTitle);
  }

  function getChapterContent(bookTitle,chapterTitle)
  {
    var readonly="";
    var editor="";
    BookDatabase.isChapterEdited(bookTitle,chapterTitle,{
      async:false,
      callback:function(isEdited)
      {
        if(isEdited!=null)
        {
          readonly="readonly";
```

```
          editor=isEdited;
        }
      }
    });
    BookDatabase.getChapterContent(bookTitle,chapterTitle,{
      callback:function(chapterContent)
      {
        var editChapterArea=dwr.util.byId('editChapterArea');
        var html='<h3>'+chapterTitle+'</h3>';
        if(editor!="")
        {
          html+='Edited by '+editor+'<br/>';
        }
        html+='<textarea '+readonly+' id="chapterContentTextArea"
         rows="10" cols="60">'+chapterContent+'</textarea><br/>';
        if(readonly=="")
        {
          html+='<input type="button" value="Save"
           onclick="saveChapterContent(\''+bookTitle+'\',
                                  \''+chapterTitle+'\');">';
          html+='<input type="button" value="Cancel"
           onclick="cancelChapterContentEdit(\''+bookTitle+'\',
                                      \''+chapterTitle+'\');">';
        }
        else
        {
          html+='<input type="button" value="Cancel" onclick=
            "closeChapterContentEdit();">';

        }
        editChapterArea.innerHTML=html;
      }
    });
    return false;
}

function cancelChapterContentEdit(bookTitle,chapterTitle)
{
      BookDatabase.cancelChapterEdit(bookTitle,chapterTitle);
      var editChapterArea=dwr.util.byId('editChapterArea');
      editChapterArea.innerHTML='';
      return false;
}
```

```
function closeChapterContentEdit()
{
    var editChapterArea=dwr.util.byId('editChapterArea');
    editChapterArea.innerHTML='';
    return false;
}

function saveChapterContent(bookTitle,chapterTitle)
{
  var editChapterArea=dwr.util.byId('chapterContentTextArea');
  var content=editChapterArea.value;
  BookDatabase.saveChapterContent(bookTitle,chapterTitle,content,{
    callback:function()
    {
      setFeedback('Content saved.');
    }
    });
  return false;
}

function setFeedback(feedback)
{
  var feedbackArea=dwr.util.byId('feedbackArea');
  feedbackArea.innerHTML=(new Date())+":<br/>"+feedback;
}

function startNewBook()
{
  var bookTitle=prompt("Book title:");
  if(bookTitle!=null)
  {
    BookDatabase.addNewBook(bookTitle,refreshBookLists);
  }
  return false;
}

function addChapter(bookTitle)
{
  //dialog to ask book title
  var chapterTitle=prompt("Chapter name:");
  if(chapterTitle!=null)
  {
    BookDatabase.insertChapter(bookTitle,chapterTitle,{
      callback:function()
        {
          getChaptersForTitle(bookTitle);
```

```
      }
    });
  }
  return false;
}

function refreshBookLists()
{
  getBookLists();
}

function clearContentAreas()
{
  var area=dwr.util.byId('feedbackArea');
  area.innerHTML='';

  area=dwr.util.byId('bookTitleContentArea');
  area.innerHTML='';

  dwr.util.removeAllRows('bookChapters');

  area=dwr.util.byId('insertChapterArea');
  area.innerHTML='';

  area=dwr.util.byId('voteArea');
  area.innerHTML='';

  area=dwr.util.byId('editChapterArea');
  area.innerHTML='';
}

</script>

</head>
<body onload="showUsersOnline();">
<div id="maincontainer">

<div id="topsection">
<div class="innertube">
<h1>Book Authoring</h1>
<h4>Welcome <i><%=(String) session.getAttribute("username")%></i></h4>
</div>
</div>

<div id="contentwrapper">
<div id="contentcolumn">
<div id="bookContent" class="innertube">
<div id="feedbackArea"></div>
```

```html
<div id="bookTitleContentArea"></div>
<table cellpadding="0" cellspacing="0">
  <tbody id="bookChapters">
  </tbody>
</table>

<div id="insertChapterArea"></div>
<div id="voteArea"></div>

<div id="editChapterArea"></div>

</div>
</div>
</div>

<div id="leftcolumn">
<div class="innertube">
<table cellpadding="0" cellspacing="0">
  <thead>
    <tr>
      <td><b>Books in process</b></td>
    </tr>
  </thead>
  <tbody id="booksInProgress">
  </tbody>
  <tfoot>
    <tr>
      <td><a href="#" onclick="startNewBook();">Start new book</a>
                                                </td>
    </tr>
  </tfoot>
</table>

<table cellpadding="0" cellspacing="0">
  <thead>
    <tr>
      <td><b>Published books</b></td>
    </tr>
  </thead>
  <tbody id="publishedBooks">
  </tbody>
</table>

<table cellpadding="0" cellspacing="0">
  <thead>
    <tr>
```

```
        <td><b>Authors online</b></td>
      </tr>
    </thead>
    <tbody id="authorsOnline">
    </tbody>
</table>

<input id="logoutButton" type="button" value="Logout"
  onclick="logout();return false;"></div>

</div>

<div id="footer">Stylesheet by <a
  href="http://www.dynamicdrive.com/style/">Dynamic Drive CSS
                                          Library</a></div>

</div>
<script type="text/javascript">
getBookLists();
</script>
</body>
</html>
```

This is quite a large page since all the client-side logic is included in the JavaScript functions within this HTML page. Let's go through the page source.

At the start of the page, before declaring the DWR functions, there is a piece of Java code whose purpose is to check whether the page request is valid or not. It is done by checking the user session, and if the username is found from the session, the request is valid and if the username is not found from the session, then an empty screen is shown to the user. This is because we don't want users to go directly to the main page (when doing further development, the login page could be shown here, instead of an empty page).

After checking the user session we load the DWR scripts. We have only two Java classes in this sample application, Login and BookDatabase.

At the start of the script element, we enable reverse AJAX (Comet) for our use. The first two functions do the logout, and redirect the user to the login screen while the third function, showUsersOnline(), displays logged-in users on the left side of the screen. As we will see later, reverse AJAX is used to call this on each user's page when a new user logs into the system. The function also uses the DWR utility functions to populate tables with usernames.

The getBookLists() function calls the BookDatabase Java class and retrieves a list of books that are in progress and books that are published. It shows the lists in the HTML page's left navigation. For a book that is in progress, a link to open a chapter page is created, and for published books, a link to open the book page is created.

The `getChapters()` function calls the `getChaptersForTitle()` function, which calls the `BookDatabase` class and gets the chapter titles for the clicked book. The function also inserts the voting button for authors, and shows the current situation of votes, and shows the number of authors who have voted among the total.

The `showBook()` function retrieves a rendered book from the `BookDatabase` and shows it in the HTML page.

The function `voteforPublish()` takes the user's vote and updates the voting status of the specified book. The `refreshChapterIfVisible()` function updates the user's screen if changes happen in the book content, and the `clearChapterViewIfVisible()` function clears the contents of the book if a user is viewing it and the book is voted to be published.

The `notifyBookPublished()` function notifies the user that a book has been published and clears the book content if it is visible.

The `getChapterContent()` function shows the chapter content in the editable text area where the user can edit a chapter. If someone else is currently editing the chapter, the read-only text area is shown to the user, and the content of the area is the latest content that has been saved by the author.

The `cancelChapterContentEdit()`, `closeChapterContentEdit()`, and the `saveChapterContent()` functions correspond to the buttons with the same name in the chapter edit page. The `save` function also calls the `setFeedback()` function to show the user the time of the save event.

The `startNewBook()` and `addChapter()` functions are used to add a book or a chapter in a book. The `refreshBookLists()` function just calls the `getBookLists()` function to get the current books in the user interface. The last function, `clearContentAreas()`, clears the book content.

The rest of the page is HTML code, and the content includes the headlines and the place holders, and `div` elements, that are used by JavaScript functions.

Configuring the Web Application

Before getting to the Java code, we need to set up DWR for our web application. We copy the `dwr.jar` file to the **WEB-INF | lib** directory and set up the `web.xml` file as shown:

```
<?xml version="1.0" encoding="UTF-8"?>
<web-app xmlns:xsi="http://www.w3.org/2001/XMLSchema-instance"
xmlns="http://java.sun.com/xml/ns/javaee" xmlns:web="http://java.sun.
com/xml/ns/javaee/web-app_2_5.xsd" xsi:schemaLocation="http://java.
sun.com/xml/ns/javaee http://java.sun.com/xml/ns/javaee/web-app_2_
```

```
5.xsd" id="WebApp_ID" version="2.5">
  <display-name>DWRBookAuthoring</display-name>
 <servlet>
    <display-name>DWR Servlet</display-name>
    <servlet-name>dwr-invoker</servlet-name>
    <servlet-class>
      org.directwebremoting.servlet.DwrServlet
    </servlet-class>
    <init-param>
      <param-name>debug</param-name>
      <param-value>true</param-value>
    </init-param>
        <init-param>
    <param-name>activeReverseAjaxEnabled</param-name>
    <param-value>true</param-value>
  </init-param>

  </servlet>

  <servlet-mapping>
    <servlet-name>dwr-invoker</servlet-name>
    <url-pattern>/dwr/*</url-pattern>
  </servlet-mapping>

    <welcome-file-list>
    <welcome-file>index.html</welcome-file>
    <welcome-file>index.htm</welcome-file>
    <welcome-file>index.jsp</welcome-file>
    <welcome-file>default.html</welcome-file>
    <welcome-file>default.htm</welcome-file>
    <welcome-file>default.jsp</welcome-file>
    </welcome-file-list>
</web-app>
```

Configuration for DWR is in the dwr.xml file and is as follows:

```
<?xml version="1.0" encoding="UTF-8"?>
<!DOCTYPE dwr PUBLIC
    "-//GetAhead Limited//DTD Direct Web Remoting 2.0//EN"
    "http://getahead.org/dwr/dwr20.dtd">

<dwr>
  <allow>
```

```
    <create creator="new" javascript="Login">
      <param name="class" value="bookauthoring.Login" />
    </create>

    <create creator="new" javascript="BookDatabase">
      <param name="class" value="bookauthoring.BookDatabase" />
    </create>

  </allow>
  </dwr>
```

In the DWR configuration, there are the two Java classes that we use in this project, Login and BookDatabase.

Developing the Java Classes

There are several Java classes in the application, and we start by developing the Login class.

Login.java

The Login class handles the user login and logout and also keeps track of the logged-in users. The source code of the Login class is as follows:

```java
package bookauthoring;

import java.util.Collection;
import java.util.List;

import javax.servlet.ServletContext;
import javax.servlet.http.HttpServletRequest;
import javax.servlet.http.HttpSession;

import org.directwebremoting.ScriptSession;
import org.directwebremoting.ServerContext;
import org.directwebremoting.ServerContextFactory;
import org.directwebremoting.WebContext;
import org.directwebremoting.WebContextFactory;
import org.directwebremoting.proxy.ScriptProxy;

public class Login {

    public Login() {
    }

    public String doLogin(String userName) {
        UserDatabase userDb=UserDatabase.getInstance();
```

```
   if(!userDb.isUserLogged(userName)) {
      userDb.login(userName);
      WebContext webContext= WebContextFactory.get();
      HttpServletRequest request = webContext.
       getHttpServletRequest();
      HttpSession session=request.getSession();
      session.setAttribute(«username», userName);
      String scriptId = webContext.getScriptSession().getId();
      session.setAttribute(«scriptSessionId», scriptId);
      updateUsersOnline();
      return «mainpage.jsp»;
   }
   else {
      return «loginFailed.html»;
   }
}

public void doLogout() {
   try {
      WebContext ctx = WebContextFactory.get();
      HttpServletRequest request = ctx.getHttpServletRequest();
      HttpSession session = request.getSession();
      Util util = new Util();
      String userName = util.getCurrentUserName(session);
      UserDatabase.getInstance().logout(userName);
      session.removeAttribute("username");
      session.removeAttribute("scriptSessionId");
      session.invalidate();
   } catch (Exception e) {
      System.out.println(e.toString());
   }
   updateUsersOnline();
}

private void updateUsersOnline() {
   WebContext webContext= WebContextFactory.get();
   ServletContext servletContext = webContext.getServletContext();
   ServerContext serverContext = ServerContextFactory.
    get(servletContext);
   webContext.getScriptSessionsByPage("");
   String contextPath = servletContext.getContextPath();
   if (contextPath != null) {
      Collection<ScriptSession> sessions =
                        serverContext.getScriptSessionsByPage
                              (contextPath + "/mainpage.jsp");
```

```
        ScriptProxy proxy = new ScriptProxy(sessions);
        proxy.addFunctionCall(«showUsersOnline»);
    }
}

public List<String> getUsersOnline() {
    UserDatabase userDb=UserDatabase.getInstance();
    return userDb.getLoggedInUsers();
}
}
```

The `doLogin()` method handles the user login. Note that there is no password checking in this sample application. If the user is not already logged in, the username is added to the `UserDatabase` class (its source code is presented shortly) and the user name is added to the HTTP session. The `doLogin()` method returns the name of the page that is shown to the user, be it the main page or the login failure page.

The `doLogout()` method does the reverse, removes the username from the `UserDatabase` and from the HTTP session.

The `updateUsersOnline()` method uses reverse AJAX to update the logged-in users list in the web pages of users who are logged in. The `getUsersOnline()` method returns the list of logged-in users from the `UserDatabase` class.

UserDatabase.java

The following is the source code of the `UserDatabase` class:

```
package bookauthoring;

import java.util.List;
import java.util.Vector;

//this class holds currently logged in users
//there is no persistence
public class UserDatabase {

    private static UserDatabase userDatabase=new UserDatabase();

    private List<String> loggedInUsers=new Vector<String>();

    private UserDatabase() {
}

    public static UserDatabase getInstance() {
        return userDatabase;
    }
```

```
    public List<String> getLoggedInUsers() {
        return loggedInUsers;
    }

    public boolean isUserLogged(String userName) {
        return loggedInUsers.contains(userName);
    }

    public void login(String userName) {
        loggedInUsers.add(userName);
    }

    public void logout(String userName) {
        loggedInUsers.remove(userName);
    }
}
```

The UserDatabase class is a very simple singleton that keeps track of only the logged-in users in a List object. There is no persistence, but it could be added easily in this class.

Util.java

The Util class is used by the Login class, and it provides helper methods for the sample application.

```
package bookauthoring;

import java.util.Hashtable;
import java.util.Map;

import javax.servlet.http.HttpServletRequest;
import javax.servlet.http.HttpSession;

import org.directwebremoting.WebContext;
import org.directwebremoting.WebContextFactory;

public class Util {

    public Util() {

    }

    public String getCurrentUserName() {
        //get user name from session
```

```
        WebContext ctx = WebContextFactory.get();
        HttpServletRequest request = ctx.getHttpServletRequest();
        HttpSession session=request.getSession();
        return getCurrentUserName(session);
    }

    public String getCurrentUserName(HttpSession session) {
        String userName=(String)session.getAttribute("username");
        return userName;
    }
}
```

The two methods, getCurrentUserName() and getCurrentUserName(HttpSession), are used for getting the usernames from an HTTP session, and they are used in various places in the application. So it makes sense to introduce a utility class for them.

Book.java

The Book class is the actual book object that gets populated when we write the book. This class holds the book title, authors, and so on.

The source code for the Book class is as follows:

```java
package bookauthoring;

import java.util.Collection;
import java.util.LinkedHashMap;
import java.util.List;
import java.util.Map;
import java.util.Vector;

public class Book {

    private String title="";
    private List<String> authors=new Vector<String>();
    private Map<String,String> chapters=new LinkedHashMap
                                    <String,String>();

    private List<String> votesForPublish=new Vector<String>();

    private boolean isPublished=false;

    public Book() {

    }
```

```java
    public void insertChapter(String chapterTitle,
                              String chapterContent) {
        chapters.put(chapterTitle, chapterContent);
    }

    public Collection<String> getChapterTitles() {
        return chapters.keySet();
    }

    public String getChapter(String chapterTitle) {
        return chapters.get(chapterTitle);
    }

    public void addAuthor(String author) {
        if(!authors.contains(author)){
            authors.add(author);
        }
    }

    public List<String> getAuthors() {
        return authors;
    }

    public int getNumberOfAuthors() {
        return authors.size();
    }

    public int getNumberOfVotes() {
        return votesForPublish.size();
    }

    public void voteForPublish(String author) {
        if(authors.contains(author)) {
            if(!votesForPublish.contains(author)) {
                votesForPublish.add(author);
                if(votesForPublish.size()==authors.size()) {
                    isPublished=true;
                }
            }
        }
    }

    public boolean isPublished() {
        return isPublished;
    }

    public boolean haveIVoted(String author) {
        return votesForPublish.contains(author);
    }
```

```
public String getTitle() {
   return title;
}

public void setTitle(String title) {
   this.title = title;
}

public String toString() {
   StringBuffer sb=new StringBuffer();
   sb.append("<h1>");
   sb.append(getTitle());
   sb.append("</h1>");
   sb.append("<p><b>Authors: </b><i>");
   for(String author : getAuthors()) {
      sb.append(author);
      sb.append(';');
   }
   sb.append("</i></p>");
   for (String title : getChapterTitles()) {
      sb.append("<h3>");
      sb.append(title);
      sb.append("</h3>");
      sb.append(getChapter(title));
   }
   return sb.toString();
}
}
```

The Book class has fields for authors (a List), a Map that holds all the chapters (implementation of the Map is ordered LinkedHashMap) and also fields for votes and a boolean to indicate whether or not the book is published. The toString() method returns the rendered book content ready for viewing in the web page.

BookDatabase.java

The actual book database is the BookDatabase class. It has methods that are remoted and used by the JavaScript function in the mainpage.jsp file. All the logic is in the class, and its source code is as follows:

```
package bookauthoring;

import java.util.Collection;
import java.util.Hashtable;
import java.util.LinkedHashMap;
import java.util.List;
import java.util.Map;
```

```java
import java.util.Vector;

import javax.servlet.ServletContext;

import org.directwebremoting.ScriptSession;
import org.directwebremoting.ServerContext;
import org.directwebremoting.ServerContextFactory;
import org.directwebremoting.WebContext;
import org.directwebremoting.WebContextFactory;
import org.directwebremoting.proxy.ScriptProxy;

public class BookDatabase {

    private static Map<String, Book> booksInProgress = new
LinkedHashMap<String, Book>();
    private static Map<String, Book> publishedBooks = new
LinkedHashMap<String, Book>();
    private static Map<String, String> editedChapters = new
Hashtable<String, String>();

    public BookDatabase() {
    }

    public List<String> getBooksInProgressTitles() {
        return getTitles(booksInProgress.values());
    }

    public List<String> getPublishedBookTitles() {
        return getTitles(publishedBooks.values());
    }

    public Collection<String> getChapters(String bookTitle) {
        Book book = getBook(bookTitle);
        if (book != null) {
            return book.getChapterTitles();
        }
        return null;
    }

    public String isChapterEdited(String bookTitle,
                                  String chapterTitle)
    {
        String isEdited = editedChapters.get(bookTitle + chapterTitle);
        return isEdited;
    }

    public void cancelChapterEdit(String bookTitle,String chapterTitle)
    {
        editedChapters.remove(bookTitle + chapterTitle);
    }
```

```java
    public List<String> getAuthors(String bookTitle) {
        Book book = getBook(bookTitle);
        if (book != null) {
            return book.getAuthors();
        }

        return null;
    }

    private List<String> getTitles(Collection<Book> books) {
        List<String> titles = new Vector<String>();
        for (Book book : books) {
            titles.add(book.getTitle());
        }
        return titles;
    }

    private Book getBook(String bookTitle) {
        return getBook(bookTitle, false);
    }

    private Book getBook(String bookTitle, boolean
                         getGromPublishedBook)
    {
        if (getGromPublishedBook) {
            if (publishedBooks.containsKey(bookTitle)) {
                return publishedBooks.get(bookTitle);
            }
        } else {
            if (booksInProgress.containsKey(bookTitle)) {
                return booksInProgress.get(bookTitle);
            }
        }
        return null;
    }

    public void addNewBook(String title) {
        if (!booksInProgress.containsKey(title)) {
            Book newBook = new Book();
            newBook.setTitle(title);
            String userName = (new Util()).getCurrentUserName();
            newBook.addAuthor(userName);
            booksInProgress.put(title, newBook);
            refreshBookList();
        }
    }
```

```
public void insertChapter(String bookTitle, String chapterTitle) {
   Book book = getBook(bookTitle);
   if (book != null) {
      String userName = (new Util()).getCurrentUserName();
      if (!book.getAuthors().contains(userName)) {
         book.addAuthor(userName);
      }
      book.insertChapter(chapterTitle, "");
      refreshChapterIfVisible(bookTitle);
   }
}

public String getChapterContent(String bookTitle, String
                                               chapterTitle)
{

   Book book = getBook(bookTitle);
   String content = "";
   if (book != null) {
      content = book.getChapter(chapterTitle);
      if (content == null) {
         content = "";
      }
   }
   String key = bookTitle + chapterTitle;
   if (!editedChapters.containsKey(key)) {
      editedChapters.put(key, (new Util()).getCurrentUserName());
   }

   return content;
}

public void saveChapterContent(String bookTitle,
                     String chapterTitle, String content)
 {
   Book book = getBook(bookTitle);
   if (book != null) {
      String userName = (new Util()).getCurrentUserName();
      if (!book.getAuthors().contains(userName)) {
         book.addAuthor(userName);
      }
      book.insertChapter(chapterTitle, content);
   }
}

public boolean amIAuthor(String bookTitle) {
   Book book = getBook(bookTitle);
   if (book != null) {
```

```
          String userName = (new Util()).getCurrentUserName();
          return book.getAuthors().contains(userName);
       }
       return false;
    }

    public boolean haveIVoted(String bookTitle) {
       Book book = getBook(bookTitle);
       if (book != null) {
          String userName = (new Util()).getCurrentUserName();
          return book.haveIVoted(userName);
       }
       return false;
    }

    public int getNumberOfAuthors(String bookTitle) {
       Book book = getBook(bookTitle);
       if (book != null) {
          return book.getAuthors().size();
       }
       return 0;
    }

    public int getNumberOfVotes(String bookTitle) {
       Book book = getBook(bookTitle);
       if (book != null) {
          return book.getNumberOfVotes();
       }
       return 0;
    }

    public void voteForPublish(String bookTitle) {
       Book book = getBook(bookTitle);
       if (book != null) {
          String userName = (new Util()).getCurrentUserName();
       book.voteForPublish(userName);
          if (book.isPublished()) {
             informBookPublished(bookTitle);
             booksInProgress.remove(bookTitle);
             publishedBooks.put(bookTitle, book);
             refreshBookList();
          }
          refreshChapterIfVisible(bookTitle);
       }
    }
```

```
   public String getRenderedBook(String bookTitle) {
      Book book = getBook(bookTitle, true);
      if (book != null) {
         return book.toString();
      }
      return "";
   }

   private ScriptProxy getScriptProxyForSessions() {
      WebContext webContext = WebContextFactory.get();
      ServletContext servletContext = webContext.getServletContext();
      ServerContext serverContext = ServerContextFactory.
                                    get(servletContext);
      webContext.getScriptSessionsByPage("");
      String contextPath = servletContext.getContextPath();
      if (contextPath != null) {
         Collection<ScriptSession> sessions = serverContext
            .getScriptSessionsByPage(contextPath +
                                    "/mainpage.jsp");
         ScriptProxy proxy = new ScriptProxy(sessions);
         return proxy;
      }
      return null;
   }

   public void refreshBookList() {
      ScriptProxy proxy =getScriptProxyForSessions();
      if(proxy!=null) {
         proxy.addFunctionCall(«getBookLists»);
      }
   }

   public void refreshChapterIfVisible(String bookTitle) {
      ScriptProxy proxy =getScriptProxyForSessions();
      if(proxy!=null) {
         proxy.addFunctionCall("refreshChapterIfVisible", bookTitle);
      }
   }

   public void informBookPublished(String bookTitle) {
      ScriptProxy proxy =getScriptProxyForSessions();
      if(proxy!=null) {
         proxy.addFunctionCall("notifyBookPublished", bookTitle);
      }
   }
}
```

The `BookDatabase` class has three static `Map` variables: `booksInProgress`, `publishedBooks`, and `editedChapters`. These hold the current state of the Book Authoring system about which books are in progress, and which have been published. Note that the books are not persistent.

The `getBooksInProgressTitles()` and `getPublishedBookTitles()` methods use the `getTitles()` method that takes a `Collection` of books and extracts title names from the `Book` objects and returns a `List` of titles to the browser.

The `getChapters()` method returns the `Collection` of chapter titles in a specified `Book` object.

The `isChapterEdited()` method checks whether a specified chapter in a specified book is currently being edited by a user or not. If the chapter is not being edited, the method returns null.

The `cancelChapterEdit()` method removes a chapter from the edited chapters list.

The `getAuthors()` method returns a `List` of authors of a specified book.

The `getBook()` method returns a `Book` object either from `booksInProgress List` or `publishedBooks List`.

The `addNewBook()` and `insertChapter()` methods start a new book or insert a new chapter to an existing book, and also update the necessary variables and use reverse AJAX to notify all the browsers about the changes.

The `getChapterContent()` method returns the chapter contents and marks the chapter as being edited if no one is editing it currently. The `saveChapterContent()` method saves the chapter and updates the author list if necessary.

The `amIAuthor()` method checks whether or not the current user is one of the book authors.

The `haveIVoted()`, `getNumberOfAuthors()`, and `voteForPublish()` methods are used to check if the user has already voted and to vote for publishing, in which case the user interface is updated using reverse AJAX about the new voting status.

The `getRenderedBook()` method returns the rendered book content. Rendering of the book happens in the `Book` object's `toString()` method.

The `getScriptProxyForSessions()` method is used in reverse AJAX, and it returns the DWR object `ScriptProxy` for all the users in the main page of the application. The `ScriptProxy` object is used to call a named JavaScript function in the main page.

The `refreshBookList()`, `refreshChapterIfVisible()`, and `informBookPublished()` methods call the JavaScript functions in the main page and notify relevant changes to the users who have logged in to the application.

Testing Collaborative Book Authoring

Now our **Book Authoring** sample application is ready for testing. The test scenario we use here is a use case where two authors log into the system and work on the same book. The following screenshots show how Collaborative Book Authoring works in practice.

Two users, **Smith** and **Brown**, are authoring the same book. The login screen is where the user enters his or her name and enters the main page of the sample application.

Smith logs in first and sees the following page:

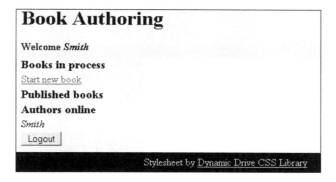

The **Authors online** table shows only **Smith** at first, and when **Brown** logs in, then Smith's screen is updated with a new username in the **Authors online** table as is shown in the following screenshot:

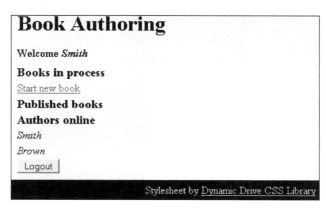

Now that Brown has logged in, he starts a new book. He clicks the **Start new book** link and a dialog box pops up asking for the name of the book.

After **Brown** enters the name, the **Books in progress** list is updated in both the browsers. Smith can now see the new book in progress in the following screenshot:

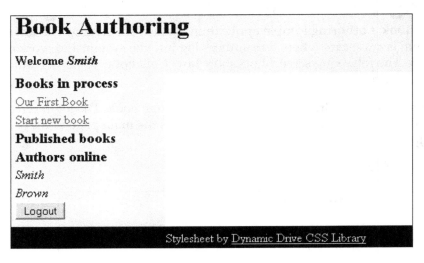

Smith clicks the **Our First Book** link, and a screen with the list of chapters opens, and he can see that Brown is currently the only author of this book.

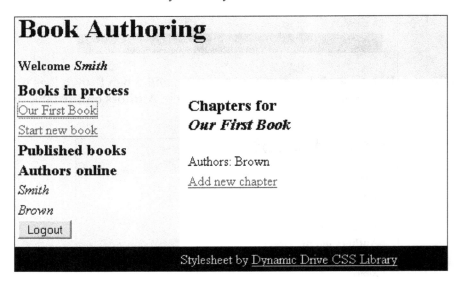

Smith decides to start a new chapter. He clicks the **Add new chapter** link and enters the name of the chapter.

Now both the users can see that there is only one chapter in the book, and because Smith has added a chapter, he is also listed as the author. Both users now have now the voting button. The following screenshot illustrates the current situation:

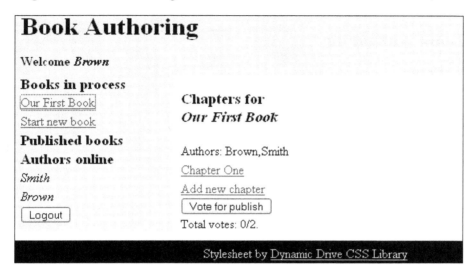

Brown decides to edit **Chapter One** and he clicks the link to open the chapter and edit the chapter as shown in the following screenshot:

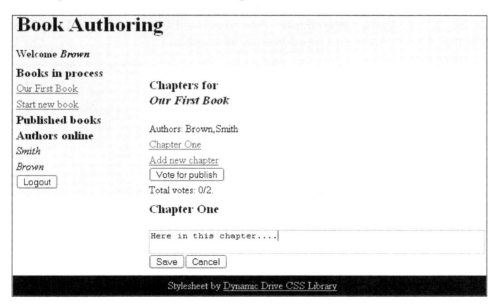

While Brown is editing, Smith also wants to edit the same chapter. He also clicks the chapter link but he cannot edit because he sees that Brown is editing the chapter at the same time. The chapter content is still empty because Brown has not saved the chapter yet.

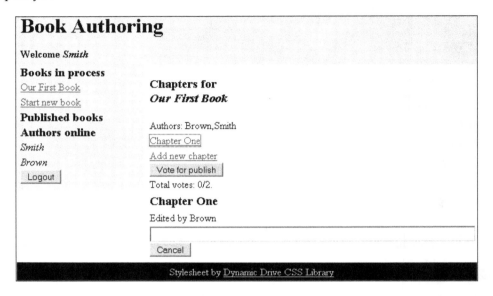

Smith cancels the edit and at the same time, Brown saves the chapter. A little later, Smith decides to edit the same chapter. Now he can edit the chapter and sees the content that Brown wrote and he adds some new content.

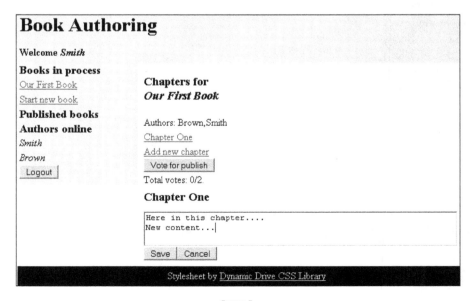

This way, two users can author the same book and when it is ready, authors can vote to publish it.

Two chapters have been added, and Brown has already voted for publishing. Smith clicks the **Vote for publish** button and is informed that he cannot take back his vote. Because Brown already voted, and there are only two authors in this book, the book will be published and moved to the **Published books** table on the left navigation.

All logged-in users get the notification that a book has been published as shown in the following screenshot:

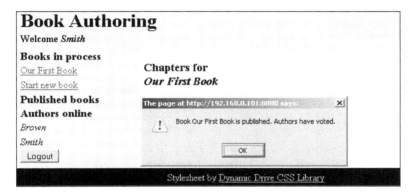

When the user clicks **OK** in the dialog box, the user interface is updated to reflect the published book. When viewing a published book, it is rendered to HTML for better viewing similar to the following screenshot:

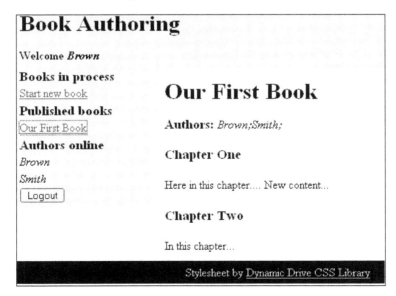

Afterword

This sample application—Collaborative Book Authoring—showed how to use DWR to create interactive multi-user applications.

Although the application shows only the basic features of collaborative possibilities, it is quite clear that without DWR and its reverse AJAX features, this kind of application would be difficult to write.

Chatroom

The Chatroom sample application is a very typical multi-user chatroom. The functionalities of this sample include a list of online users, automatic refresh of chat text, and the ability to send messages to the chat room.

Some of the code here is taken directly from the previous Book Authoring sample. Only the package names have been changed while the rest of the code is basically just copy-pasted to a new class

Re-use by copy-paste is not a recommended practice, but it is done here in order to keep these samples self-contained without dependencies to other samples.

Starting the Project and Configuration

We start by creating a new project for our chat room, with the project name DWRChatRoom. We also need to add the `dwr.jar` file to the **lib** directory and enable DWR in the `web.xml` file. The following is the source code of the `dwr.xml` file.

```xml
<?xml version="1.0" encoding="UTF-8"?>
<!DOCTYPE dwr PUBLIC
    "-//GetAhead Limited//DTD Direct Web Remoting 2.0//EN"
    "http://getahead.org/dwr/dwr20.dtd">

<dwr>
  <allow>
    <create creator="new" javascript="Login">
      <param name="class" value="chatroom.Login" />
    </create>
    <create creator="new" javascript="ChatRoomDatabase">
      <param name="class" value="chatroom.ChatRoomDatabase" />
    </create>

  </allow>
  </dwr>
```

The source code for web.xml is as follows:

```xml
<?xml version="1.0" encoding="UTF-8"?>
<web-app xmlns:xsi="http://www.w3.org/2001/XMLSchema-instance"
xmlns="http://java.sun.com/xml/ns/javaee" xmlns:web="http://java.sun.
com/xml/ns/javaee/web-app_2_5.xsd" xsi:schemaLocation="http://java.
sun.com/xml/ns/javaee http://java.sun.com/xml/ns/javaee/web-app_2_
5.xsd" id="WebApp_ID" version="2.5">
  <display-name>DWRChatRoom</display-name>
<servlet>
    <display-name>DWR Servlet</display-name>
    <servlet-name>dwr-invoker</servlet-name>
    <servlet-class>
      org.directwebremoting.servlet.DwrServlet
    </servlet-class>
    <init-param>
      <param-name>debug</param-name>
      <param-value>true</param-value>
    </init-param>
    <init-param>
      <param-name>activeReverseAjaxEnabled</param-name>
      <param-value>true</param-value>
    </init-param>
  </servlet>
  <servlet-mapping>
    <servlet-name>dwr-invoker</servlet-name>
    <url-pattern>/dwr/*</url-pattern>
  </servlet-mapping>

  <welcome-file-list>
    <welcome-file>index.html</welcome-file>
    <welcome-file>index.htm</welcome-file>
    <welcome-file>index.jsp</welcome-file>
    <welcome-file>default.html</welcome-file>
    <welcome-file>default.htm</welcome-file>
    <welcome-file>default.jsp</welcome-file>
  </welcome-file-list>
</web-app>
```

Developing the User Interface

The next step we do is to create files for presentation: style sheet and HTML/JSP files. Here, we re-use files from the previous DWRBookAuthoring sample. The syle sheet is the same, loginFailed.html is the same and index.jsp has only one change, and that is the title of the page. These pages are not presented here, and their functionality is described in the previous section.

The main page, `mainpage.jsp`, includes all the client-side logic of our ChatRoom application. The source code for the page is as follows:

```
<!DOCTYPE html PUBLIC "-//W3C//DTD XHTML 1.0 Transitional//EN"
  "http://www.w3.org/TR/xhtml1/DTD/xhtml1-transitional.dtd">
<html xmlns="http://www.w3.org/1999/xhtml" lang="en" xml:lang="en">
<head>
<meta http-equiv="Content-Type" content="text/html; charset=iso-8859-
1" />
<title>Chatroom</title>
<link href="styles.css" rel="stylesheet" type="text/css" />
<%
    if (session.getAttribute("username") == null
            || session.getAttribute("username").equals("")) {
        //if not logged in and trying to access this page
        //do nothing, browser shows empty page
        return;
    }
%>
<script type='text/javascript' src='/DWRChatRoom/dwr/interface/Login.
js'></script>
<script type='text/javascript' src='/DWRChatRoom/dwr/interface/
ChatRoomDatabase.js'></script>
<script type='text/javascript' src='/DWRChatRoom/dwr/engine.js'></
script>
<script type='text/javascript' src='/DWRChatRoom/dwr/util.js'></
script>

<script type="text/javascript">
dwr.engine.setActiveReverseAjax(true);

function logout()
{
  Login.doLogout(showLoginScreen);
}

function showLoginScreen()
{
  window.location.href='index.jsp';
}

function showUsersOnline()
{
  var cellFuncs = [
          function(user) {
```

```
                return '<i>'+user+'</i>';
            }
            ];
    Login.getUsersOnline({
    callback:function(users)
    {
      dwr.util.removeAllRows('usersOnline');
      dwr.util.addRows( "usersOnline",users, cellFuncs,
                        { escapeHtml:false });
    }
    });
}

function getPreviousMessages()
{
    ChatRoomDatabase.getChatContent({
    callback:function(messages)
    {
      var chatArea=dwr.util.byId('chatArea');
      var html="";
      for(index in messages)
      {
          var msg=messages[index];
          html+=msg;
      }
      chatArea.innerHTML=html;
      var chatAreaHeight = chatArea.scrollHeight;
      chatArea.scrollTop = chatAreaHeight;
    }
    });

}

function newMessage(message)
{
  var chatArea=dwr.util.byId('chatArea');
  var oldMessages=chatArea.innerHTML;
  chatArea.innerHTML=oldMessages+message;
  var chatAreaHeight = chatArea.scrollHeight;
  chatArea.scrollTop = chatAreaHeight;
}

function sendMessageIfEnter(event)
{
  if(event.keyCode == 13)
```

```
    {
      sendMessage();
    }
  }

  function sendMessage()
  {
      var message=dwr.util.byId('messageText');
      var messageText=message.value;
      ChatRoomDatabase.postMessage(messageText);
      message.value='';
  }
  </script>
  </head>
  <body onload="showUsersOnline();">
  <div id="maincontainer">

  <div id="topsection">
  <div class="innertube">
  <h1>Chatroom</h1>
  <h4>Welcome <i><%=(String) session.getAttribute("username")%></i></h4>
  </div>
  </div>

  <div id="contentwrapper">
  <div id="contentcolumn">
  <div id="chatArea" style="width: 600px; height: 300px; overflow:
  auto">
  </div>
  <div id="inputArea">
  <h4>Send message</h4>
  <input id="messageText" type="text" size="50"
        onkeyup="sendMessageIfEnter(event);">
  <input type="button" value="Send msg" onclick="sendMessage();">
  </div>
  </div>
  </div>

  <div id="leftcolumn">
  <div class="innertube">

  <table cellpadding="0" cellspacing="0">
    <thead>
      <tr>
        <td><b>Users online</b></td>
```

```
       </tr>
    </thead>
    <tbody id="usersOnline">
    </tbody>
</table>

<input id="logoutButton" type="button" value="Logout"
    onclick="logout();return false;"></div>

</div>

<div id="footer">Stylesheet by
    <a href="http://www.dynamicdrive.com/style/">
            Dynamic Drive CSS Library</a></div>
</div>
<script type="text/javascript">
getPreviousMessages();
</script>

</body>
</html>
```

The functionality at the beginning of the page is the same as in the `mainpage.jsp` page in the previous DWRBookAuthoring sample.

The first chat-room-specific JavaScript function is `getPreviousMessages()`. This function is called at the end of `mainpage.jsp`, and it retrieves previous chat messages for this chat room.

The `newMessage()` function is called by the server-side Java code when a new message is posted to the chat room. The function also scrolls the chat area automatically to show the latest message.

The `sendMessageIfEnter()` and `sendMessage()` functions are used to send user messages to the server. There is the input field for the message text in the HTML code, and the `sendMessageIfEnter()` function listens to `onkeyup` events in the input field. If the user presses enter, the `sendMessage()` function is called to send the message to the server.

The HTML code includes the chat area of specified size and with automatic scrolling.

Developing the Java Code

The Java code for the chat room sample uses the same classes as the DWRBookAuthoring sample. The `Login`, `UserDatabase` and `Util` classes are the same except that the package name is different. The logic for the server-side chat room functionality is in the `ChatRoomDatabase` class. The source code for the `ChatRoomDatabase` is as follows:

```
package chatroom;

import java.util.Collection;
import java.util.Date;
import java.util.List;
import java.util.Vector;

import javax.servlet.ServletContext;

import org.directwebremoting.ScriptSession;
import org.directwebremoting.ServerContext;
import org.directwebremoting.ServerContextFactory;
import org.directwebremoting.WebContext;
import org.directwebremoting.WebContextFactory;
import org.directwebremoting.proxy.ScriptProxy;

public class ChatRoomDatabase {

    private static List<String> chatContent = new Vector<String>();

    public ChatRoomDatabase() {
    }

    public void postMessage(String message) {
        String user = (new Util()).getCurrentUserName();
        if (user != null) {
            Date time = new Date();
            StringBuffer sb = new StringBuffer();
            sb.append(time.toString());
            sb.append(" <b><i>");
            sb.append(user);
            sb.append("</i></b>:   ");
            sb.append(message);
            sb.append("<br/>");
            String newMessage=sb.toString();
            chatContent.add(newMessage);
            postNewMessage(newMessage);
        }
    }

    public List<String> getChatContent() {
        return chatContent;
    }

    private ScriptProxy getScriptProxyForSessions() {
        WebContext webContext = WebContextFactory.get();
        ServletContext servletContext = webContext.getServletContext();
        ServerContext serverContext = ServerContextFactory.
get(servletContext);
        webContext.getScriptSessionsByPage("");
        String contextPath = servletContext.getContextPath();
        if (contextPath != null) {
```

```
        Collection<ScriptSession> sessions =
                    serverContext.getScriptSessionsByPage
                                (contextPath + "/mainpage.jsp");
        ScriptProxy proxy = new ScriptProxy(sessions);
        return proxy;
    }
    return null;
}

public void postNewMessage(String newMessage) {
    ScriptProxy proxy = getScriptProxyForSessions();
    if (proxy != null) {
        proxy.addFunctionCall(«newMessage»,newMessage);
    }
}
}
```

The Chatroom code is surprisingly simple. The chat content is stored in a Vector of Strings. The getChatContent() method just returns the chat content Vector to the browser.

The postMessage() method is called when the user sends a new chat message. The method verifies whether the user is logged in, and adds the current time and username to the chat message and then appends the message to the chat content.

The method also calls the postNewMessage() method that is used to show new chat content to all logged-in users. Note that the postMessage() method does not return any value. We let DWR and reverse AJAX functionality show the chat message to all users, including the user who sent the message.

The getScriptProxyForSessions() and postNewMessage() methods use reverse AJAX to update the chat areas of all logged-in users with the new message.

And that is it! The chat room sample is very straightforward and basic functionality is already in place, and the application is ready for further development.

Testing the Chat

We test the chat room application with three users: Smith, Brown, and Jones. We have given some screenshots of a typical scenario in a chat room here.

Both Smith and Brown log into the system and exchange some messages. Both users see empty chat rooms when they log in and start chatting.

The empty area that is above the send message input field is reserved for chat content. **Smith** and **Brown** exchange some messages as is seen in the following screenshot:

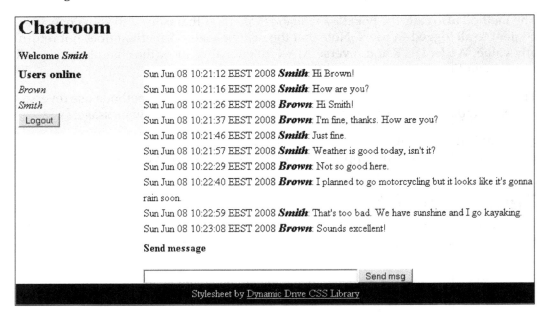

The third user, Jones, joins the chat and sees all the previous messages in the chat room. Jones then exchanges some messages with Smith and Brown. Smith and Brown log out from the system leaving Jones alone in the chat room (until she also logs out). This is visible in the following screenshot:

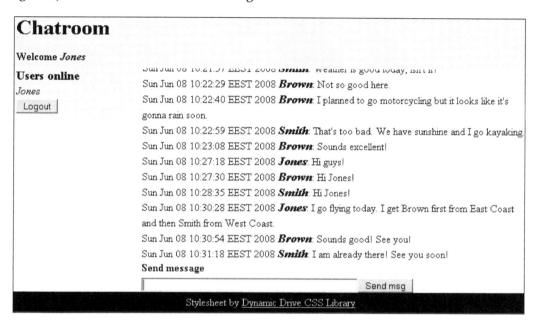

Afterword

This sample application showed how to use DWR in a chat room application. The functionality is similar to the previous Book Authoring application.

Summary

The two sample applications, Collaborative Book Authoring and Chatroom, presented in this chapter make it clear that DWR makes development of these kind of collaborative applications very easy.

DWR itself does not even play a big part in the applications. DWR is just a transparent feature of the application. So developers concentrate on the actual project and aspects such as persistence of data and a neat user interface, instead of the low-level details of AJAX.

Index

AJAX and PHP

ISBN: 190-4-811-82-5   Paperback: 275 pages

Enhance the user experience of your PHP website using AJAX with this practical tutorial featuring detailed case studies

1. Build a solid foundation for your next generation of web applications

2. Use better JavaScript code to enable powerful web features

3. Leverage the power of PHP and MySQL to create powerful back-end functionality and make it work in harmony with the smart AJAX client

Google Web Toolkit

ISBN: 978-1-847191-00-7   Paperback: 240 pages

A practical guide to Google Web Toolkit for creating AJAX applications with Java, fast.

1. Create rich Ajax applications in the style of Gmail, Google Maps, and Google Calendar

2. Interface with Web APIs create GWT applications that consume web services

3. Completely practical with hands-on examples and complete tutorials right from the first chapter

Please check **www.PacktPub.com** for information on our titles

www.ingramcontent.com/pod-product-compliance
Lightning Source LLC
Chambersburg PA
CBHW060549060326
40690CB00017B/3656